22 Foundation designs to challenge you... kills!

Best of Fons&Porter
paper-pieced QUILTS

LEISURE ARTS
the art of everyday living
www.leisurearts.com

FONS & PORTER STAFF
Editors-in-Chief Marianne Fons and Liz Porter

Editor Jean Nolte
Associate Editor Diane Tomlinson
Technical Editor Marjon Schaefer
Technical Writer Kristine Peterson

Art Director Tony Jacobson

Interactive Editor Mandy Couture
Sewing Specialist Cindy Hathaway

Contributing Photographers Dean Tanner, Katie Downey, Craig Anderson
Contributing Photo Assistant DeElda Wittmack

Publisher Kristi Loeffelholz
Advertising Manager Cristy Adamski
Retail Manager Sharon Hart
Web Site Manager Phillip Zacharias
Customer Service Manager Tiffiny Bond
Fons & Porter Staff Megan Johansen, Laura Saner, Yvonne Smith, Anne Welker, Karla Wesselmann

New Track Media LLC
President and CEO Stephen J. Kent
Chief Financial Officer Mark F. Arnett
President, Book Publishing W. Budge Wallis
Vice President/Publishing Director Joel P. Toner
Vice President/Group Publisher Tina Battock
Vice President, Circulation Nicole McGuire
Vice President, Production Barbara Schmitz
Production Manager Dominic M. Taormina
IT Manager Denise Donnarumma
Renewal and Billing Manager Nekeya Dancy
Online Subscriptions Manager Jodi Lee

Our Mission Statement
Our goal is for you to enjoy making quilts as much as we do.

LEISURE ARTS STAFF
Vice President of Editorial Susan White Sullivan
Creative Art Director Katherine Laughlin
Special Projects Director Susan Frantz Wiles
Prepress Technician Stephanie Johnson

President and Chief Executive Officer Rick Barton
Senior Vice President of Operations Jim Dittrich
Vice President of Finance Fred F. Pruss
Vice President of Sales-Retail Books Martha Adams
Vice President of Mass Market Bob Bewighouse
Vice President of Technology and Planning Laticia Mull Dittrich
Controller Francis Caple
Information Technology Director Brian Roden
Director of E-Commerce Mark Hawkins
Manager of E-Commerce Robert Young
Retail Customer Service Manager Stan Raynor

Library of Congress Control Number: 2013907772
ISBN-13/EAN: 978-1-4647-0870-1

We're thrilled to bring you this collection of some of our very favorite paper-pieced quilts! The projects we've included are among our most popular of all time. You'll find challenging as well as easier foundation-pieced projects of all sizes. Enjoy the beautiful photography as you browse through the pages to find the quilt that's just right for you. Whether you prefer traditional or contemporary fabrics, you'll find plenty to love. You'll also appreciate our trademarked *Sew Easy* lessons that will guide you via step-by-step photography through any project-specific special techniques. We think you'll have fun stitching these beautiful quilts to use in your home or to give as gifts to family and friends.

Happy quilting,

Marianne & Liz

Table of Contents

72

120

42

82

64

86

Isabella

Designer Toby Lischko used several fun techniques in this quilt.
Fussy-cut centers, foundation-pieced points, and curved piecing for the arcs
all contribute to her unique design.

PROJECT RATING: CHALLENGING

Size: 56½" × 76½"

MATERIALS

2¼ yards black border print for border #4

1⅛ yards large black print for blocks

⅝ yard small black print for binding

1½ yards medium cream print for blocks and border #1

2½ yards light cream print for background and border #3

⅜ yard green print for blocks

⅜ yard brown print for blocks

⅝ yards wine print for blocks and border #2

1½ yards rust print for blocks

Paper for foundation piecing

Template material

4½ yards backing fabric

Twin-size quilt batting

Cutting

Measurements include ¼" seam allowances. Border strips are exact length needed. You may want to make them longer to allow for piecing variations. Patterns are on pages 11–13. For instructions on paper foundation piecing, see *Sew Easy: Paper Foundation Piecing* on page 37.

From black border print, cut:

• 4 (4¾"-wide) **lengthwise** strips, centering design in each.

From large black print, cut:

• 1 (4⅞"-wide) strip. From strip, cut 8 (4⅞") squares. Cut squares in half diagonally to make 16 half-square B triangles.

• 16 F, fussy cut in 4 matching sets of 4. See *Sew Easy: Fussy Cutting* on page 11.

From small black print, cut:

• 8 (2¼"-wide) strips for binding.

From medium cream print, cut:

• 9 (2½"-wide) strips. From 6 strips, cut 2 (2½" × 40½") top and bottom border #1 and 32 (2½" × 4½") A rectangles. Piece remaining strips to make 2 (2½" × 60½") side border #1.

• 8 I.

• 8 I reversed.

From light cream print, cut:

• 8 (4"-wide) strips. From strips, cut 96 (4" × 3") D rectangles for foundation piecing.

• 1 (4⅞"-wide) strip. From strip, cut 8 (4⅞") squares. Cut squares in half diagonally to make 16 half-square B triangles.

• 3 (2½"-wide) strips. From 2 strips, cut 16 (2½" × 4½") A rectangles. Remaining strip is for strip set.

• 1 (2"-wide) strip. From strip, cut 4 (2") J squares.

• 6 (1"-wide) strips. Piece strips, to make 2 (1" × 67½") side border #3 and 2 (1" × 48½") top and bottom border #3.

• 8 I.

• 8 I reversed.

From green print, cut:

• 2 (4"-wide) strips. From strips, cut 32 (4" × 2") E rectangles for foundation piecing.

From brown print, cut:

• 2 (4"-wide) strips. From strips, cut 32 (4" × 2") E rectangles for foundation piecing.

From wine print, cut:

• 1 (4"-wide) strip. From strip, cut 16 (4" × 2") E rectangles for foundation piecing.

- 1 (2½"-wide) strip. From strip, cut 4 (2½") C squares.
- 6 (2"-wide) strips. Piece strips to make 2 (2" × 64½") side border #2 and 2 (2" × 44½") top and bottom border #2.

From rust print, cut:

- 2 (2½"-wide) strips. From 1 strip, cut 8 (2½") C squares. Remaining strip is for strip set.
- 16 H.
- 16 G.

Block 1 Assembly

1. Join 1 light cream print strip and 1 rust print strip as shown in *Strip Set Diagram*. From strip set, cut 16 (2½"-wide) segments.

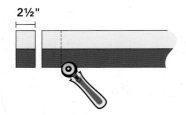

Strip Set Diagram

2. Join 1 segment and 1 light cream print A rectangle as shown in *Corner Unit Diagrams*. Make 16 Corner Units.

Corner Unit Diagrams

3. Join 1 large black print B triangle and 1 light cream print B triangle as shown in *Triangle-Square Diagrams*. Make 16 triangle-squares.

Triangle-Square Diagrams

4. Lay out 2 Corner Units, 2 triangle-squares, 4 medium cream print A rectangles, and 1 rust print C square as shown in *Block 1 Assembly Diagram*. Join into rows; join rows to complete 1 Block 1 *(Block 1 Diagram)*. Make 8 Block 1.

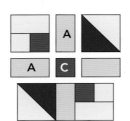

Block 1 Assembly Diagram

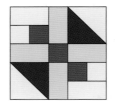

Block 1 Diagram

Block 2 Assembly

1. Trace or photocopy 16 Point Unit foundations.

2. Foundation piece Point Units in numerical order, using green, brown, and wine print E rectangles and light cream print D rectangles. Make 16 Point Units *(Point Unit Diagram)*.

Point Unit Diagram

3. Join 1 medium cream print I and 1 light cream print I reversed as shown in *Block Background Diagrams*. Make 8 block backgrounds.

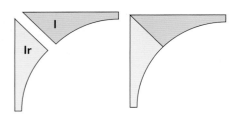

Block Background Diagrams

4. In the same manner, make 8 block backgrounds using light cream print I and medium cream print I reversed.

5. Lay out 1 black print F, 1 rust print G, 1 Point Unit, 1 rust print H, and 1 block background as shown in *Block 2 Assembly Diagram*. Join to complete 1 Block 2 *(Block 2 Diagram)*. Make 16 Block 2.

Block 2 Assembly Diagram

Block 2 Diagram

Sew Smart™

Lay out 4 Block 2 at a time, carefully matching sets of F, and paying attention to placement of light cream and medium cream in block backgrounds. —Liz

Quilt Assembly

1. Lay out blocks as shown in *Quilt Top Assembly Diagram*. Join into rows; join rows to complete quilt center.

Quilt Top Assembly Diagram

Finishing

1. Divide backing into 2 (2¼-yard) lengths. Cut 1 piece in half length-wise to make 2 narrow panels. Join 1 narrow panel to each side of wider panel; press seam allowances toward narrow panels.

2. Layer backing, batting, and quilt top; baste. Quilt as desired. Quilt shown was quilted with scalloped leaves in the background, leaf designs in the rings and border #2, and outline quilting around flowers in border #4 (*Quilting Diagram*).

3. Join 2¼"-wide small black print strips into 1 continuous piece for straight-grain French-fold binding. Add binding to quilt.

Quilting Diagram

2. Add 1 side border #1 to each side of quilt center. Add 1 wine print C square to each end of top and bottom border #1. Add borders to quilt.

3. Add 1 side border #2 to each side of quilt. Add 1 light cream print J square to each end of top and bottom border #2. Add borders to quilt.

4. Add 1 side border #3 to each side of quilt. Add top and bottom border #3 to quilt.

5. Mark center of each border #4 and each side of quilt. Pin borders to quilt top, matching centers.

6. Add borders to quilt, mitering corners.

> For Instructions on mitering borders, see *Sew Easy: Mitered Borders* on page 67.

TRIED & TRUE

This design is also pretty in pastels. We used fabrics from the Nana's Garden collection by Arlene Neely of Rabbits Haven for Red Rooster Fabrics.

DESIGNER

Toby Lischko is an award-winning quilter who designs her own quilts and has her own line of patterns. She's been quiting since 1985, and teaching quilting workshops since 1995. Look for Toby's book, *St. Louis Stars*, published by Kansas City Star. ✳

Fussy Cutting

Use this easy method to cut identical pieces from a print fabric.

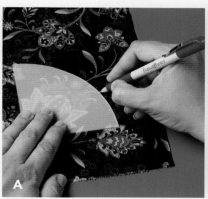

1. Make plastic template for quarter circle (F) right.

2. Position template atop fabric motif *(Photo A)*. Draw around template and cut on line or cut around template with rotary cutter.

3. Place fabric piece atop fabric, right sides up and aligning design on piece with fabric below. When properly aligned, you will barely be able to see cut piece *(Photo B)*.

4. Cut around fabric (pattern) piece with scissors to make identical piece *(Photo C)*. Be careful not to cut pattern piece.

5. Repeat to cut required number of pieces.

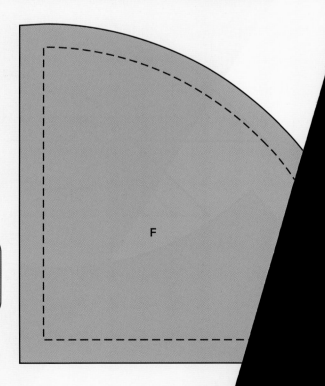

Sew **Smart**™
Always use the same piece for the pattern so pieces don't get progressively bigger. —Liz

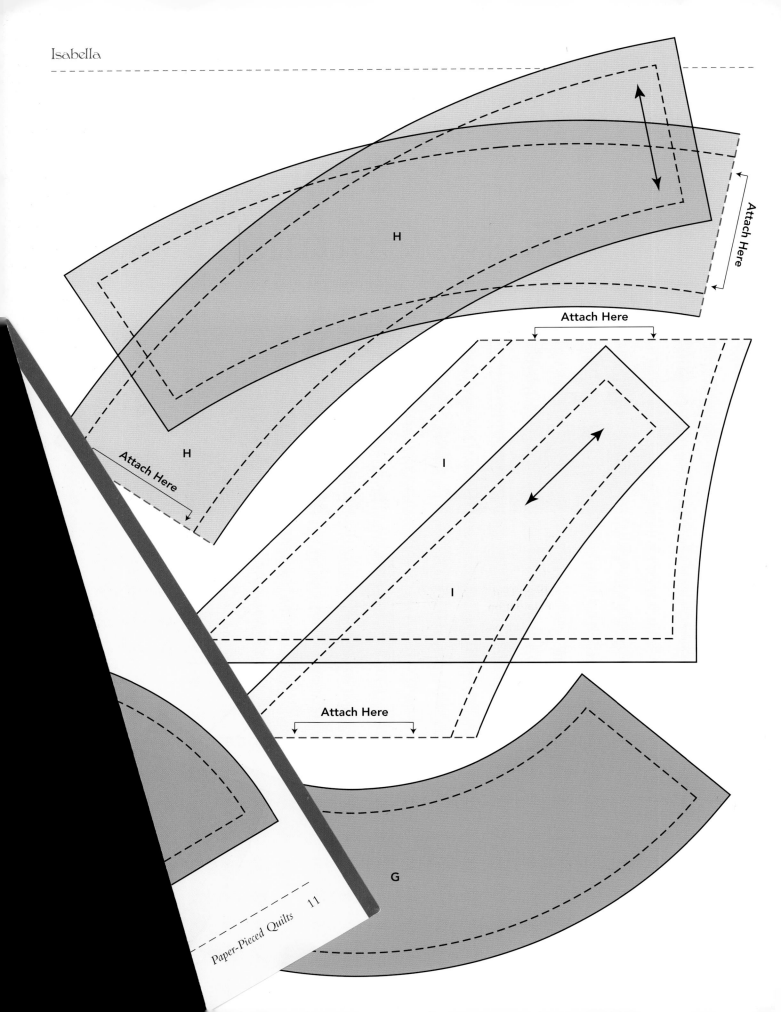

H

Attach Here

Attach Here

H

Attach Here

Attach Here

I

I

Attach Here

G

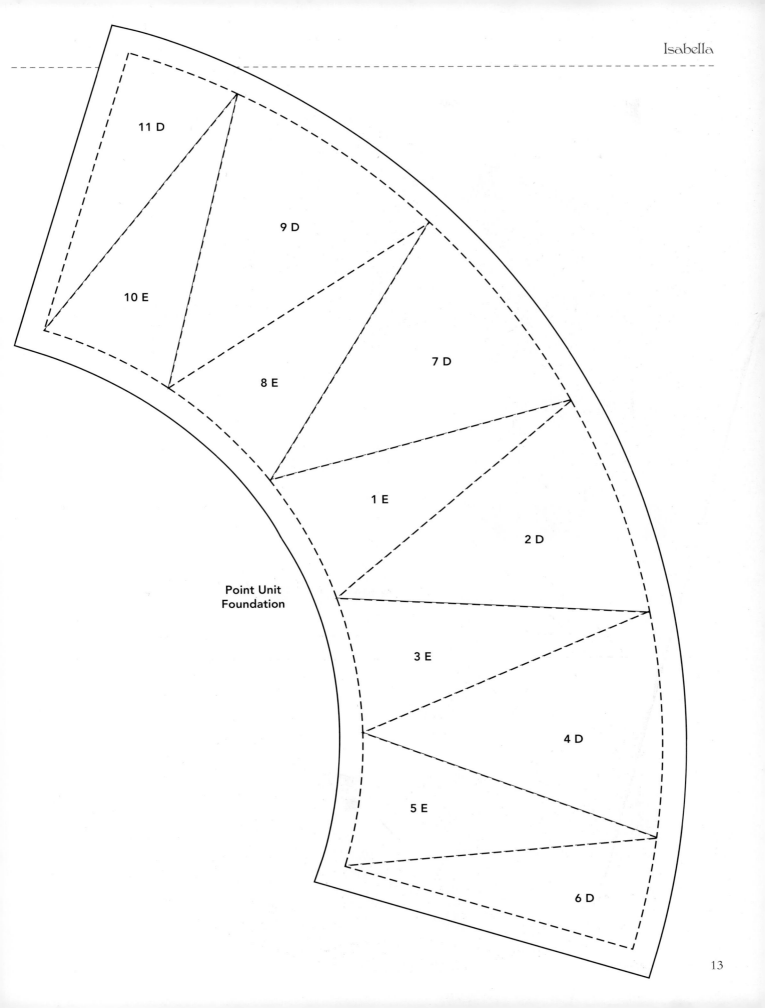

11 D

9 D

10 E

8 E

7 D

1 E

2 D

**Point Unit
Foundation**

3 E

4 D

5 E

6 D

Times Square

The brilliant lights of Times Square at night inspired Diane Tomlinson to make this magnificent foundation-pieced New York Beauty quilt.

PROJECT RATING: CHALLENGING
Size: 86" × 98"
Blocks:
151 (6") New York Beauty blocks
66 (4") Square-in-a-Square blocks

MATERIALS

7 yards light blue batik for blocks and outer border
3½ yards medium blue batik for blocks
5 yards dark blue batik for outer border and binding
2½ yards pink batik for blocks
¾ yard each of 9 assorted green batiks for blocks
¾ yard each of 8 assorted purple batiks for blocks
½ yard each of 6 assorted orange batiks for blocks
7⅞ yards backing fabric
Queen-size quilt batting

Cutting

Measurements include ¼" seam allowances. Border strips are exact length needed. You may want to make them longer to allow for piecing variations. Patterns for templates, Arc, Border, and Square-in-a Square foundations are on pages 20–21. Pieces for foundation piecing are cut oversize.
NOTE: Since there are so many pieces that are similar in size, you may want to label them as you cut.

Web **Extra**

For instructions and a video on foundation piecing, go to
www.FonsandPorter.com/pfp

From light blue batik, cut:
• 102 F.
• 202 (3½") squares for foundation piecing (Arc Unit A pieces A3 and A5).
• 202 (3½" × 2") rectangles for foundation piecing (Arc Unit A pieces A1 and A7).
• 260 (5" × 2") rectangles for foundation piecing (Border Unit pieces D2, D4, D7, D9, and D11).

From medium blue batik, cut:
• 49 F.
• 100 (3½") squares for foundation piecing (Arc Unit A pieces A3 and A5).
• 100 (3½" × 2") rectangles for foundation piecing (Arc Unit A pieces A1 and A7).
• 260 (2½") squares for foundation piecing (Arc Unit B pieces B3, B5, B7, B9, and B11).
• 104 (2½" × 2") rectangles for foundation piecing (Arc Unit B pieces B1 and B13).

From dark blue batik, cut:
• 1 (4½"-wide) strip. From strip, cut 4 (4½") G squares.
• 10 (2¼"-wide) strips for binding.
• 15 (1½"-wide) strips. Piece strips to make 2 (1½" × 76½") side border #3, 2 (1½" × 66½") top and bottom border #3, 2 (1½" × 66½") side border #1, and 2 (1½" × 56½") top and bottom border #1.
• 416 (5" × 2") rectangles for foundation piecing (Border Unit pieces D1, D3, D5, D6, D8, D10, D12, and D13).

From pink batik, cut:

- 250 (2½") squares for foundation piecing (Arc Unit B pieces B3, B5, B7, B9, and B11).
- 100 (2½" × 2") rectangles for foundation piecing (Arc Unit B pieces B1 and B13).

From assorted green batiks, cut a total of:

- 453 (3½" × 2") rectangles for foundation piecing (Arc Unit A pieces A2, A4, and A6).
- 245 (2½") squares for foundation piecing (Arc Unit B pieces B3, B5, B7, B9, and B11).
- 98 (2½" × 2") rectangles for foundation piecing (Arc Unit B pieces B1 and B13).

From assorted purple batiks, cut a total of:

- 612 (2½") squares for foundation piecing (Arc Unit B pieces B2, B4, B6, B8, B10, and B12).

From assorted orange batiks, cut a total of:

- 294 (2½") squares rectangles for foundation piecing (Arc Unit B pieces B2, B4, B6, B8, B10, and B12).

From remainders of all batiks, cut a total of:

- 151 E.
- 66 (2¼") squares for foundation piecing (Square-in-a-Square block piece C1).
- 66 pairs of matching (2¼") squares. Cut squares in half diagonally to make 264 half-square triangles for foundation piecing (Square-in-a-Square block pieces C2, C3, C4, and C5).
- 66 pairs of matching (2¾") squares. Cut squares in half diagonally to make 264 half-square triangles for foundation piecing (Square-in-a-Square block pieces C6, C7, C8, and C9).

- 66 pairs of matching (3¼") squares. Cut squares in half diagonally to make 264 half-square triangles for foundation piecing (Square-in-a-Square block pieces C10, C11, C12, and C13).

New York Beauty Block Assembly

1. Trace or photocopy 151 each of Arc Foundation Units A and B from pattern on page 20.
2. Referring to *Arc Unit A Diagrams*, paper piece foundation units in numerical order. Make 50 medium blue Arc Unit A using medium blue odd numbered A pieces and assorted green even numbered A pieces. Make 101 light blue Arc Unit A using light blue odd numbered A pieces and assorted green even numbered A pieces.

MAKE 50   MAKE 101

Arc Unit A Diagrams

3. In a similar manner, paper piece 50 pink Arc Unit B using pink odd numbered B pieces and assorted purple even numbered B pieces. Make 52 medium blue Arc Unit B using medium blue odd numbered B pieces and assorted purple even numbered B pieces. Make 49 green Arc Unit B using green odd numbered B pieces and assorted orange even numbered B pieces (*Arc Unit B Diagrams*).

MAKE 50   MAKE 52   MAKE 49

Arc Unit B Diagrams

4. Lay out 1 medium blue Arc Unit A, 1 pink Arc Unit B, 1 E, and 1 light blue F as shown in *New York Beauty Block Assembly Diagram*. Join to complete 1 pink New York Beauty block (*New York Beauty Block Diagrams*). Make 50 pink New York Beauty blocks.

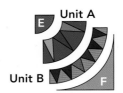

New York Beauty Block Assembly Diagram

MAKE 50   MAKE 49

MAKE 52

New York Beauty Block Diagrams

Web Extra

For instructions and video on sewing curved seams go to www.FonsandPorter.com/scurseams

5. In the same manner, make 49 green New York Beauty blocks using 1 light blue Arc Unit A, 1 green Arc Unit B, 1 E, and 1 medium blue F in each. Make 52 blue New York Beauty blocks using 1 light blue Arc Unit A, 1 medium blue Arc Unit B, 1 E, and 1 light blue F in each.

Square-in-a-Square Block Assembly

1. Trace or photocopy 66 Square-in-a-Square Block foundations from pattern on page 21.

2. Paper piece foundations in numerical order using C1 squares; matching C2, C3, C4 and C5 triangles; matching C6, C7, C8, and C9 triangles; and matching C10, C11, C12, and C13 triangles. Make 66 Square-in-a-Square blocks *(Square-in-a-Square Block Diagram)*.

Square-in-a-Square Block Diagram

Border Assembly

1. Trace or photocopy 52 Border Unit foundations from pattern on page 21.

2. Paper piece foundations in numerical order using dark blue D1, D3, D5, D6, D8, D10, D12, and D13 pieces and medium blue D2, D4, D7, D9, and D11 pieces. Make 52 Border Units *(Border Unit Diagram)*.

Border Unit Diagram

3. Referring to *Quilt Top Assembly Diagram* on page 18, join 17 Square-in-a-Square blocks to make 1 pieced side border #2. Make 2 pieced side border #2.

4. In the same manner, make pieced top border #2 using 16 Square-in-a-Square blocks. Repeat for pieced bottom border #2.

5. Join 13 medium blue New York Beauty blocks to make 1 pieced border #4. Make 4 pieced border #4.

6. Join 14 Border Units to make 1 pieced side border #5. Make 2 pieced side border #5.

7. In the same manner, make pieced top border #5 using 12 Border Units and 2 dark blue G squares. Repeat for pieced bottom border #5.

Quilt Assembly

1. Lay out pink and green New York Beauty blocks as shown in *Quilt Top Assembly Diagram*. Join into rows; join rows to complete quilt center.

2. Add dark blue side border #1 to quilt center. Add dark blue top and bottom border #1 to quilt.

3. Repeat for pieced border #2, dark blue border #3, pieced border #4, and pieced border #5.

Finishing

1. Divide backing into 3 (2⅝-yard) lengths. Join panels lengthwise. Seams will run horizontally.

2. Layer backing, batting, and quilt top; baste. Quilt as desired. Quilt shown was quilted with freehand designs in New York Beauty blocks and outer border and a spiral and meandering in Square-in-a-Square blocks *(Quilting Diagram)*.

3. Join 2¼"-wide dark blue strips into 1 continuous piece for straight-grain French-fold binding. Add binding to quilt.

Quilting Diagram

#5 G
#4
#3
#2
#1

Quilt Top Assembly Diagram

DESIGNER

Diane Tomlinson, Associate Editor of *Love of Quilting*, was so engrossed in her New York Beauty blocks, she lost track of time as she stitched—a true labor of love that is worth every minute. Diane enjoys designing quilts on her computer, changing blocks and colors until she has a pattern she loves. She likes to make intricate quilts with lots of small pieces, and has already designed her next three quilts.

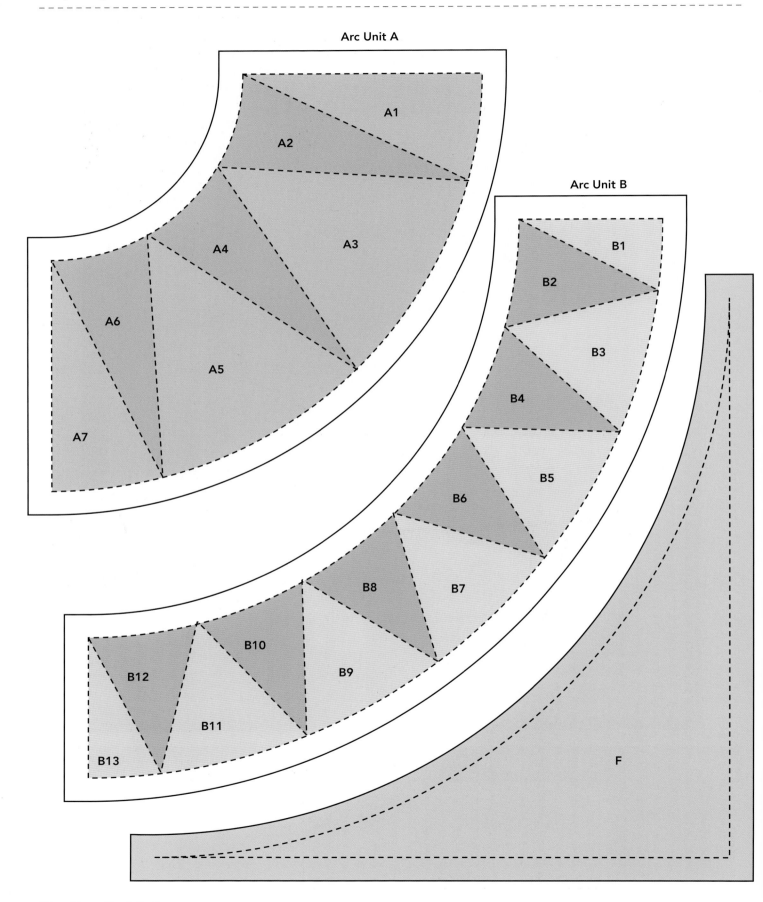

Arc Unit A

Arc Unit B

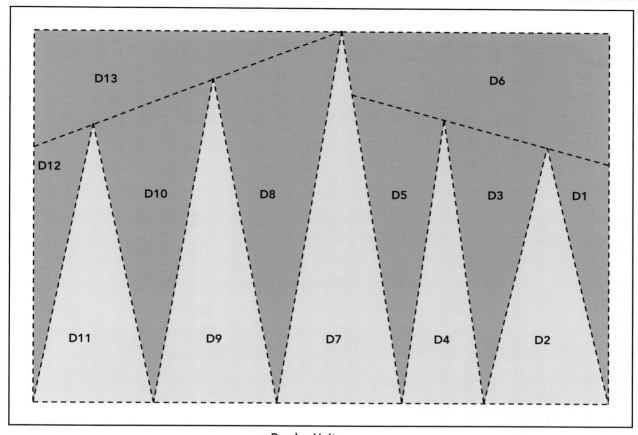

Border Unit

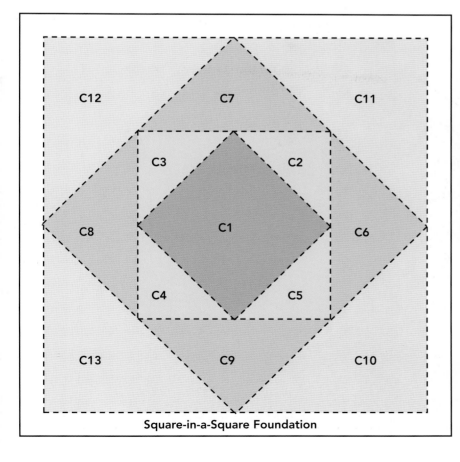

Square-in-a-Square Foundation

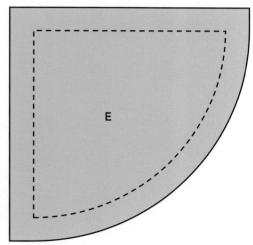

Project Linus

This quilt by Michael Michalski of Brooklyn, New York, was chosen as the first-place winner in the Artistic Category of our Project Linus Quilt Contest for its originality, design, and workmanship.

PROJECT RATING: CHALLENGING
Size: 60" × 60"

MATERIALS

¾ yard multicolor print for melons

2 yards purple print for accent strips and binding

2 yards turquoise print for inner border

1⅞ yards pink print for star foundations and outer border

1 fat quarter★ each green, turquoise, and gold prints for foundation-pieced stars

¾ yard each orange, purple, turquoise, and pink star prints for arcs

2¼ yards yellow print for arc backgrounds

Paper for foundation piecing

4 yards backing fabric

Twin-size quilt batting

★fat quarter = 18" × 20"

Cutting

Measurements include ¼" seam allowances. Foundation patterns are on pages 26–36. Instructions for paper foundation piecing are on page 37.

From multicolor print, cut:
• 16 Melons.

From purple print, cut:
• 280" of 2½"-wide bias strips. Join strips to make bias binding.
• 620" of 1"-wide bias strips.

From turquoise print, cut:
• 4 Inner Borders

NOTE: Join 8 inner border sections to make complete Inner Border pattern.

From pink print, cut:
• 8 (8"-wide) strips. From strips, cut 4 (8" × 32") rectangles and 4 (8" × 24½") rectangles. Use leftover pieces for Star foundations.

Foundation Assembly

NOTE: Star Foundation consists of 3 sections. Join pattern sections before making Star Foundation. Each small Arc consists of 2 sections. Each Large Arc consists of 7 sections.

1. Trace or photocopy 20 complete Star Foundations, 32 of each Small Arc Section, and 4 of each Large Arc Section.

2. Referring to *Star Foundation Diagram,* paper piece foundations in numerical order using green, turquoise, gold, and pink prints. Make 20 Star Foundations.

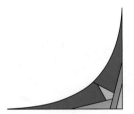

Star Foundation Diagram

> ### Sew **Smart**™
> **Machine baste inside outer seam allowance of each Star Foundation to hold fabrics in sections 2 and 4 in place. —Liz**

3. Join small arc sections to make 16 complete Small Arc Foundations. Referring to *Small Arc Foundation Diagrams,* paper piece foundations in numerical order using turquoise, purple, orange, and pink star prints and yellow print. Make 16 with pink star print in position #1 and 16 with turquoise star print in position #1.

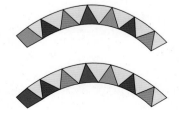

Small Arc Foundation Diagrams

4. Join 5 Large Arc Sections to make 1 Large Arc Foundation. Make 4 Large Arc Foundations.

> ### Sew **Smart**™
> **To make handling easier, Large Arcs can be pieced in sections then joined. Pay attention to color pattern as you piece sections.**
> **—Marianne**

5. Paper piece foundations using turquoise, purple, orange, and pink star prints and yellow print.

NOTE: Color pattern repeats in this order: turquoise, purple, orange, pink. Begin and end 1 Large Arc Foundation with turquoise, 1 with purple, 1 with orange, and 1 with pink.

Unit Assembly

1. Press seam allowance of one long edge of 1"-wide purple print bias toward wrong side. Place bias strip right side up atop 1 melon, aligning raw edges as shown in *Melon Diagrams.* Machine or hand appliqué pressed edge of bias strip to melon. Trim ends of strip even with edge of melon. Repeat for other side of melon. Make 16 melons.

Melon Diagrams

2. Join 1 Melon and 2 arcs as shown in *Melon/Arc Assembly Diagrams.* Make 16 Melon/Arc Units.

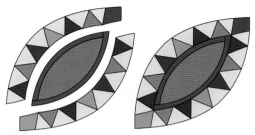

Melon Diagrams

3. Join 1 Melon/Arc Unit and 2 Star Foundations as shown in *Center Unit Diagrams.* Make 4 Center Units.

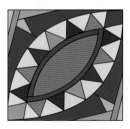

Center Unit Diagrams

4. Join 1 Melon/Arc Unit and 1 Star Foundation as shown in *Corner Unit Diagram.* Make 12 Corner Units.

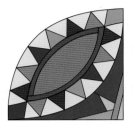

Corner Unit Diagram

Quilt Assembly

1. Add purple print bias strip to outside edge of each turquoise print inner border as described in step #1 of Unit Assembly.

2. Lay out 1 Center Unit, 3 Corner Units, 1 inner border, and 1 Large Arc as shown in *Quadrant Diagrams.* Join Center Unit and Corner Units. Add inner border and Large Arc.

3. Join 1 (8" × 32") pink print rectangle and 1 (8" × 24½") pink print rectangle as shown in *Outer Border Unit Diagrams.* Place 1 Pieced Quadrant atop Outer Border Unit as shown. Appliqué curved edge of pieced section to Outer Border Unit. Trim ends of rectangles even with ends of Large Arc to complete 1 quadrant. Make 4 Quadrants.

Outer Border Unit Diagrams

Sew **Smart**™

If you want to piece the quadrant and outer border rather than appliqué, trace curve of quadrant on Border Unit with a chalk pencil. Draw another line ½" inside traced line. Cut on inside line. Join outer border to quadrant —Liz

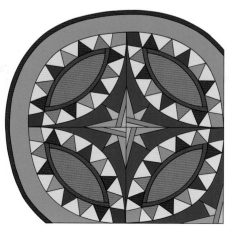

Quadrant Diagrams

4. Join quadrants as shown in *Quilt Top Assembly Diagram* to complete quilt center.

5. Trim corners of quilt in a curve, using a large bowl or other round object for a pattern.

Finishing

1. Divide backing into 2 (2-yard) lengths. Join panels lengthwise.

2. Layer backing, batting, and quilt top; baste. Quilt as desired.

3. Add binding to quilt.

Quilt Top Assembly Diagram

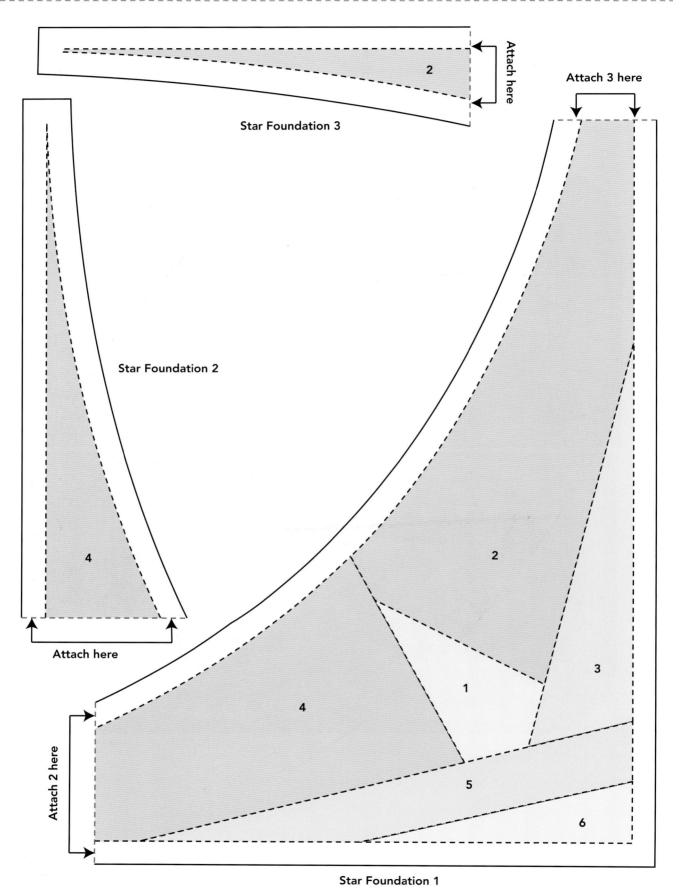

Star Foundation 3

Attach here

Attach 3 here

Star Foundation 2

2

4

Attach here

Attach 2 here

4

2

1

3

5

6

Star Foundation 1

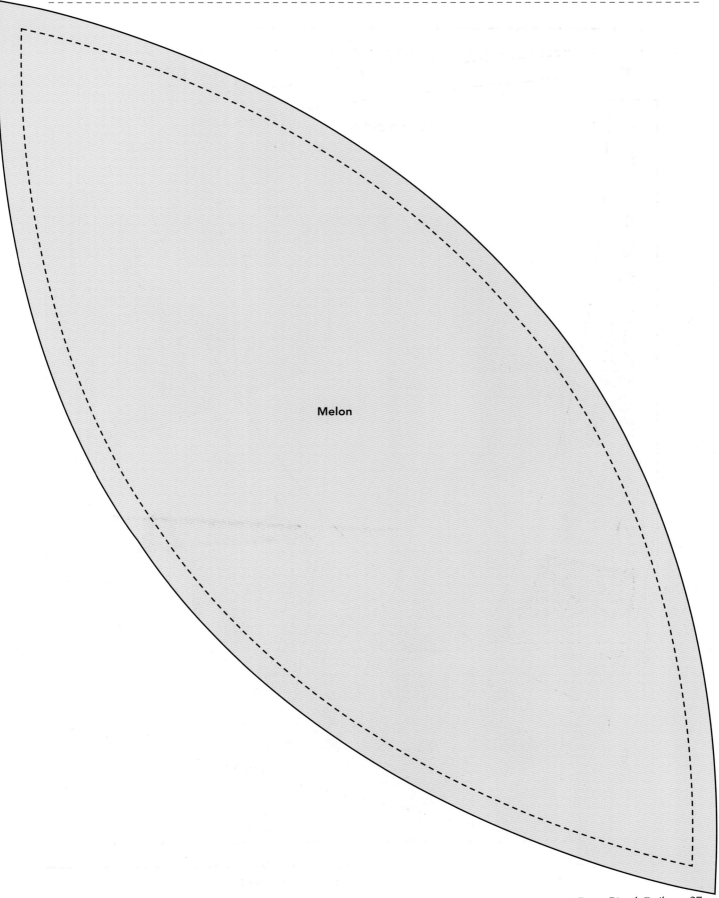

Melon

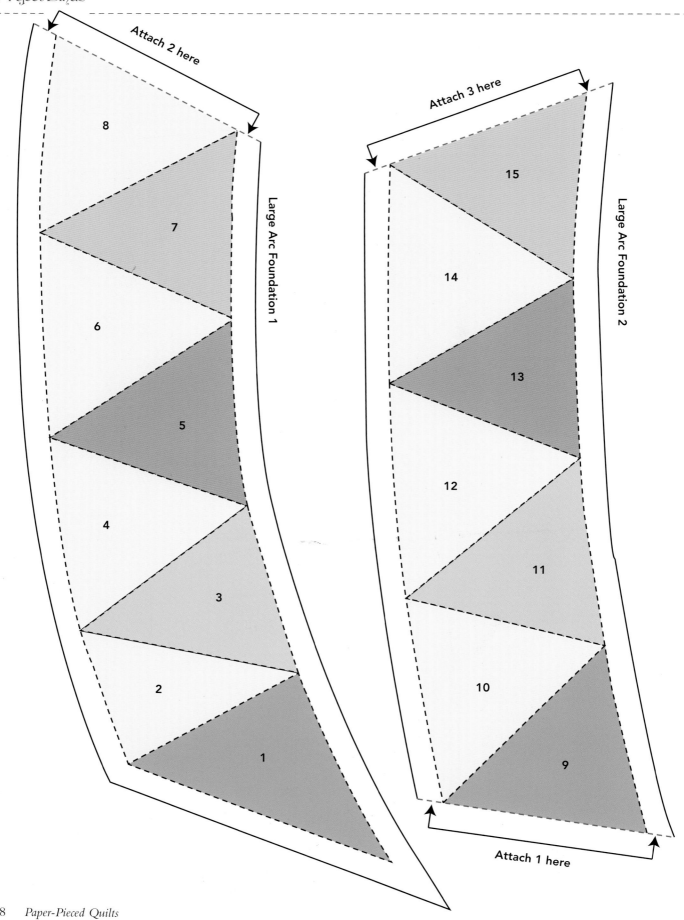

Attach 2 here

8

7

6

5

4

3

2

1

Large Arc Foundation 1

Attach 3 here

15

14

13

12

11

10

9

Large Arc Foundation 2

Attach 1 here

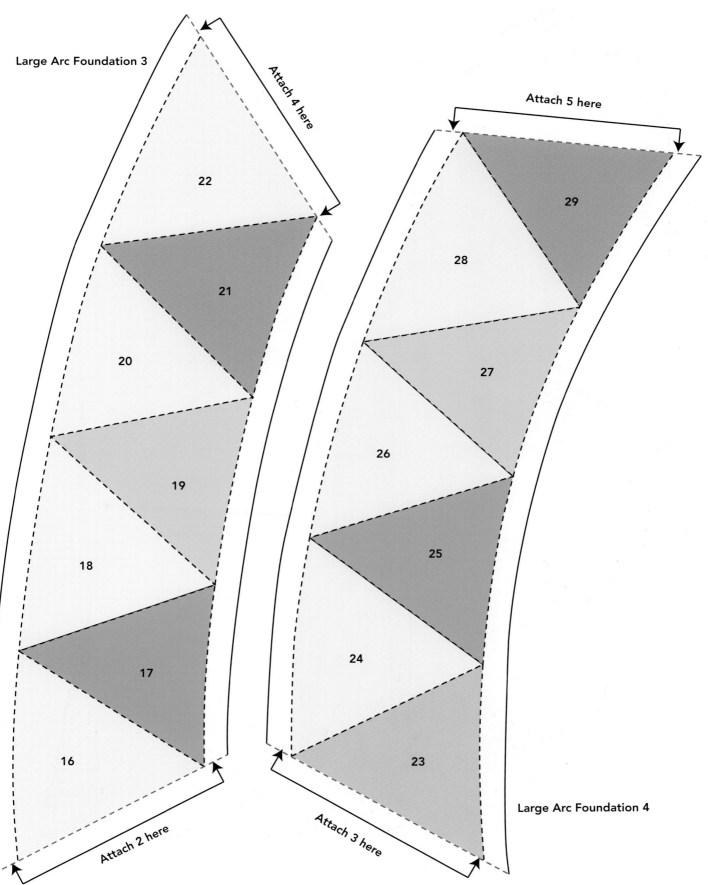

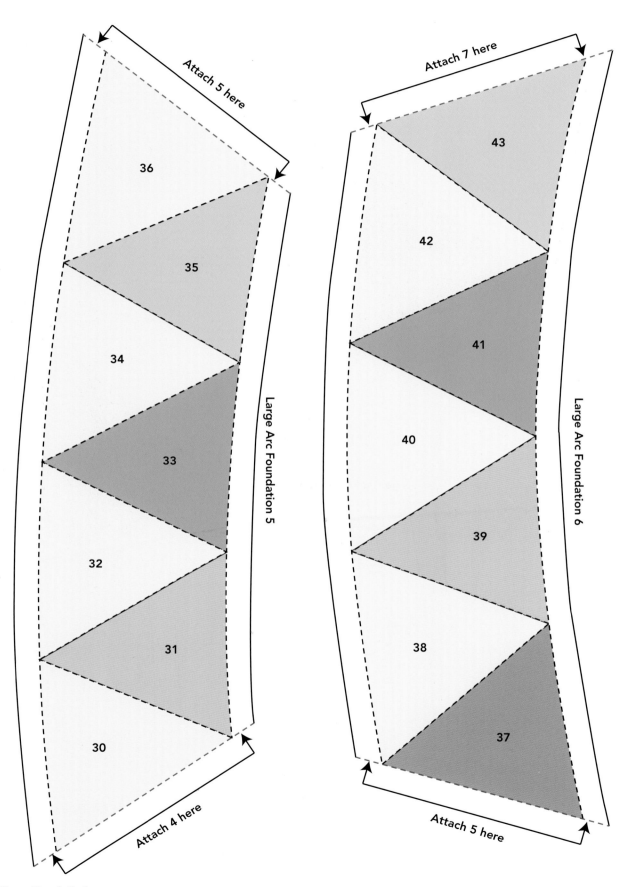

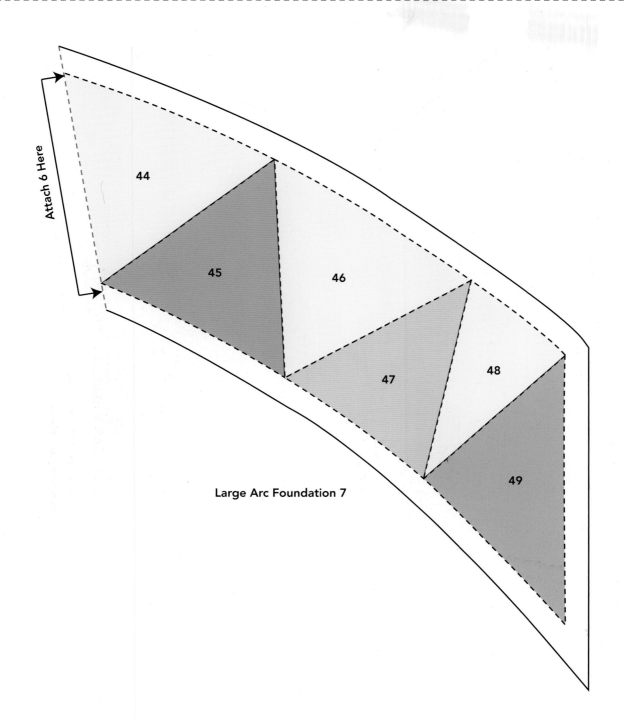

Attach 6 Here

44

45

46

47

48

49

Large Arc Foundation 7

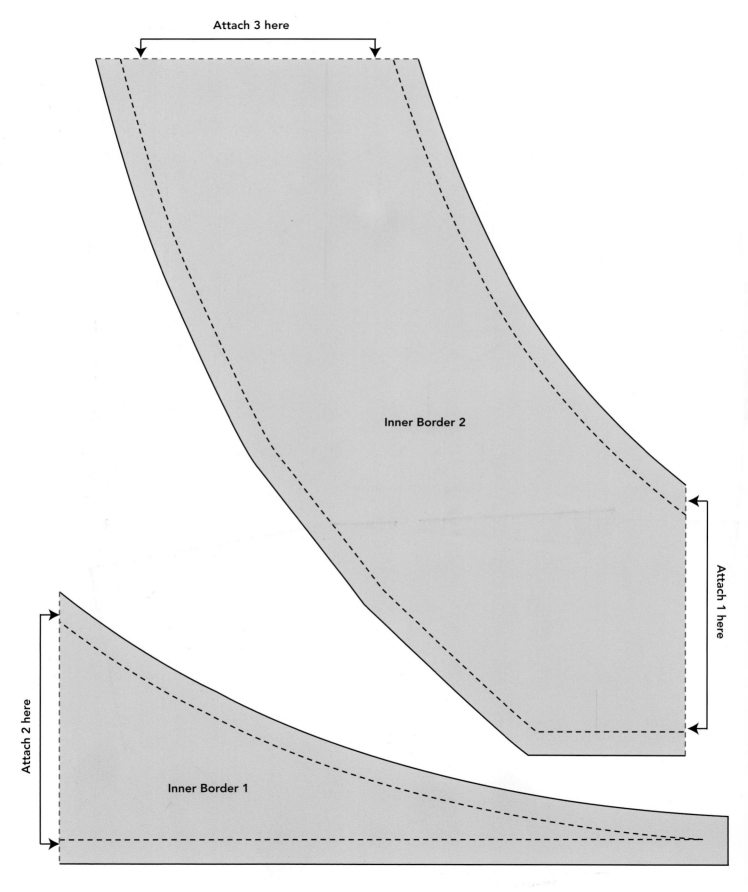

Attach 3 here

Inner Border 2

Attach 1 here

Attach 2 here

Inner Border 1

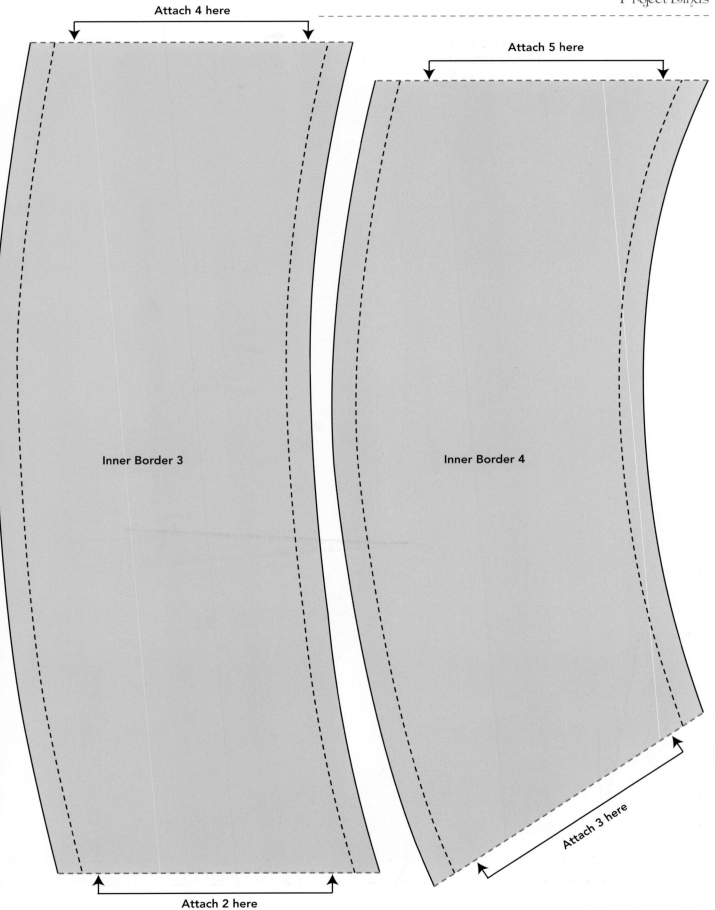

Attach 4 here

Attach 5 here

Inner Border 3

Inner Border 4

Attach 2 here

Attach 3 here

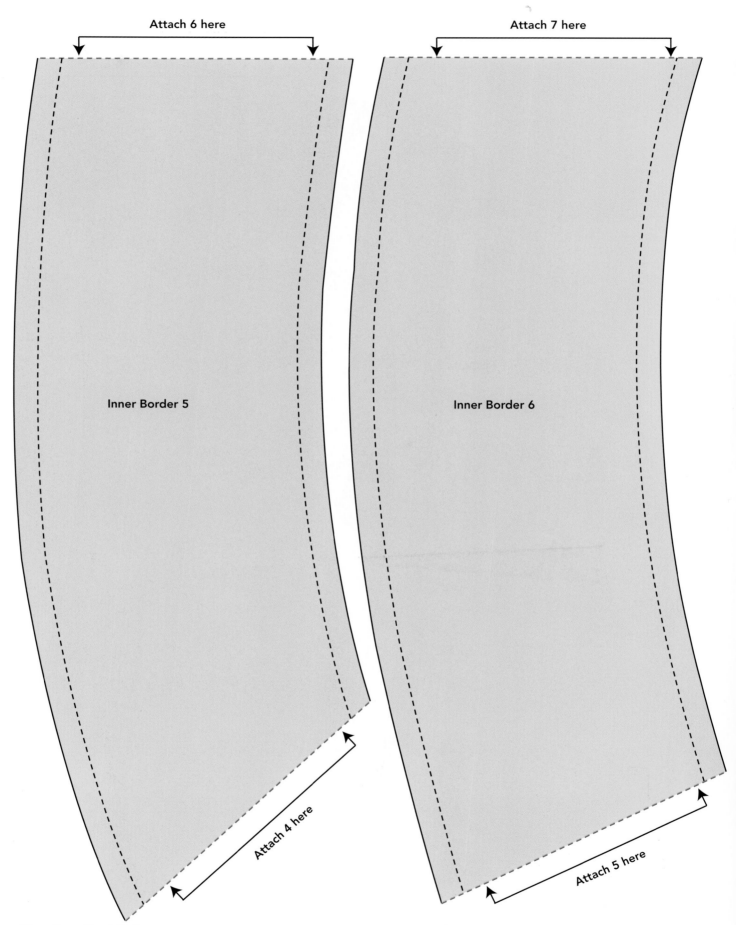

Attach 6 here

Attach 7 here

Inner Border 5

Inner Border 6

Attach 4 here

Attach 5 here

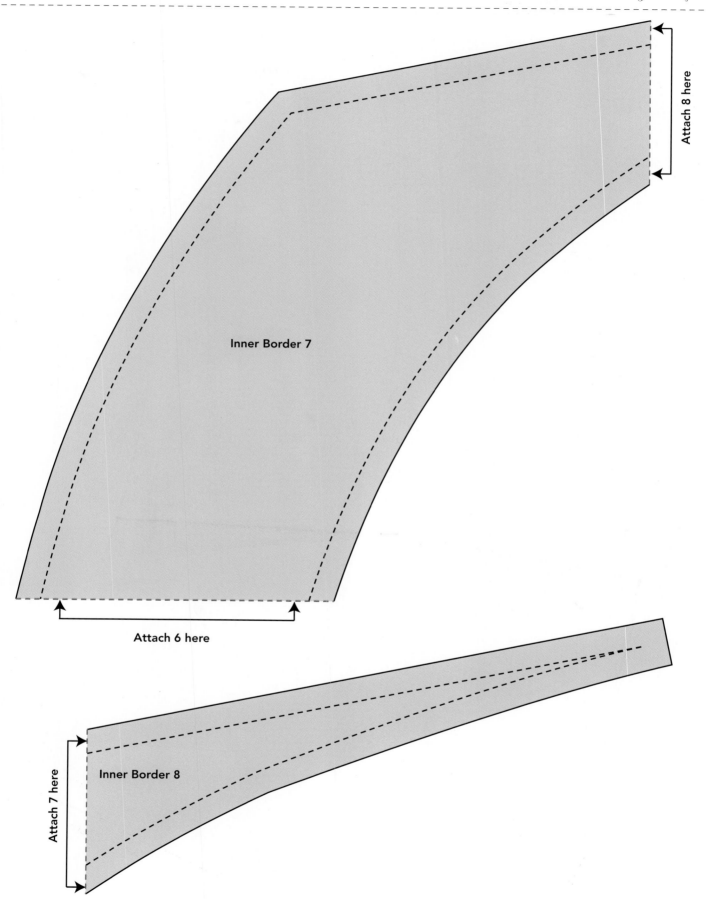

Attach 8 here

Inner Border 7

Attach 6 here

Attach 7 here

Inner Border 8

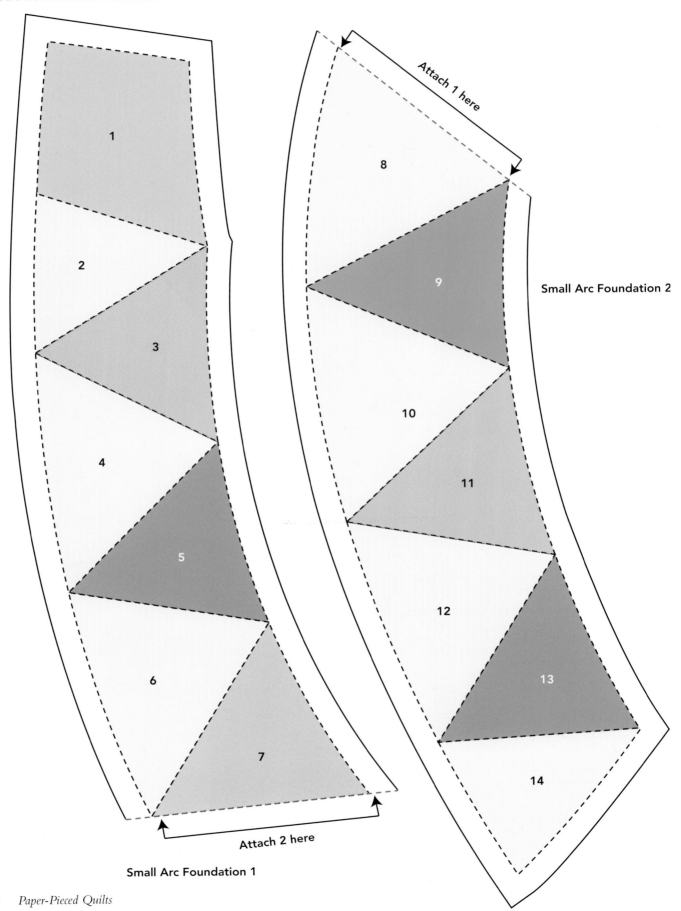

Attach 1 here

Small Arc Foundation 2

Attach 2 here

Small Arc Foundation 1

Paper Foundation Piecing

Paper foundation piecing is ideal for designs with odd angles and sizes of pieces.

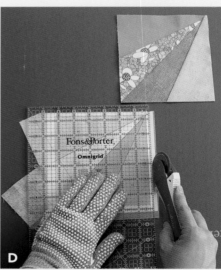

1. Using ruler and pencil, trace all lines and the outer edge of the foundation pattern onto tracing paper. Number the pieces to indicate the stitching order.

Sew Smart™

Save time by making photocopies on special foundation papers. Check photocopied patterns to be sure they are correct size. (Some copiers may distort copy size.) —Liz

2. Using fabric pieces that are larger than the numbered areas, place fabrics for #1 and #2 right sides together. Position paper pattern atop fabrics with printed side of paper facing you. Make sure the fabric for #1 is under that area and that edges of fabrics extend ¼" beyond stitching line between the two sections.

3. Using a short machine stitch so papers will tear off easily later, stitch on line between the two areas, extending stitching into seam allowances at ends of seams (*Photo A*).

4. Open out pieces and press or finger press the seam (*Photo B*). The right sides of the fabric pieces will be facing out on the back side of the paper pattern.

5. Flip the work over and fold back paper pattern on stitched line. Trim seam allowance to ¼", being careful not to cut paper pattern (*Photo C*).

6. Continue to add pieces in numerical order until pattern is covered. Use rotary cutter and ruler to trim excess paper and fabric along outer pattern lines (*Photo D*).

7. Carefully tear off foundation paper after blocks are joined.

New York Beauty

Award-winning designer Mabeth Oxenreider used paper foundation piecing
and fabrics that contrast well to create drama for the sharp points of her blocks.
The folk art colors and viny prints she chose make a spectacular quilt.

PROJECT RATING: CHALLENGING

Size: 46" × 46"

Blocks:

16 (8½") New York Beauty blocks

MATERIALS

16 fat quarters★ of assorted navy, olive, gold, rust, and cream prints for blocks

¼ yard gold stripe for inner border

1½ yards navy large-scale print for outer border and binding

3 yards backing fabric

50" square of quilt batting

Lightweight paper or stabilizer for patchwork foundations

Freezer paper for templates

★fat quarter = 18" × 20"

Cutting

Make templates for C piece and Large Take-Away Template for D piece on page 40. Make 16 tracings of arc foundation pattern on page 41 on lightweight paper or stabilizer. Measurements include ¼" seam allowances. Border strips are exact length needed. You may want to make them longer to allow for piecing variations.

From each fat quarter, cut:

• 1 (9") D square.

• 1 C piece.

• 9 (2½" × 4½") rectangles for arc background A pieces.

• 8 (1½" × 4½") rectangles for B arc points.

From gold print, cut:

• 4 (2"-wide) strips. From strips, cut 2 (34½"-long) side inner borders and 2 (37½"-long) top and bottom inner borders.

From navy large-scale floral, cut:

• 5 (5"-wide) strips. From strips, cut 2 (37½"-long) side outer borders and 2 (46½"-long) top and bottom outer borders.

• 5 (2¼"-wide) binding strips.

From gold stripe, cut:

• 4 (2"-wide) strips. From strips, cut 2 (34½"-long) side inner borders and 2 (37½"-long) top and bottom inner borders.

Block Assembly

Following instructions in *Sew Easy: Piecing New York Beauty Blocks* on page 44, make 16 blocks *(Block Diagram)*. Use assorted fabrics for each block.

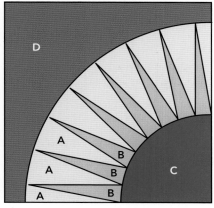

Block Diagram

Quilt Assembly

1. Referring to photo below, lay out blocks in 4 rows with 4 blocks in each row.

2. Join blocks into rows; join rows.

3. Join side inner borders to quilt. Add top and bottom borders. Repeat for outer borders.

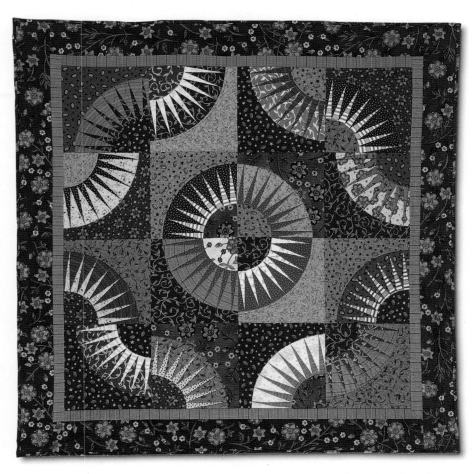

Quilting and Finishing

1. Divide backing fabric into 2 (1½-yard) pieces. Divide 1 panel in half lengthwise. Join 1 narrow panel to wide panel. Remaining panel is extra and may be used to make a hanging sleeve.

2. Layer backing, batting, and quilt top; baste. Quilt as desired. Quilt shown was quilted ¼" from curved arc seams and with meander quilting in C and D pieces and borders.

3. Join 2¼"-wide navy print strips into 1 continuous piece for straight-grain French-fold binding. Add binding to quilt.

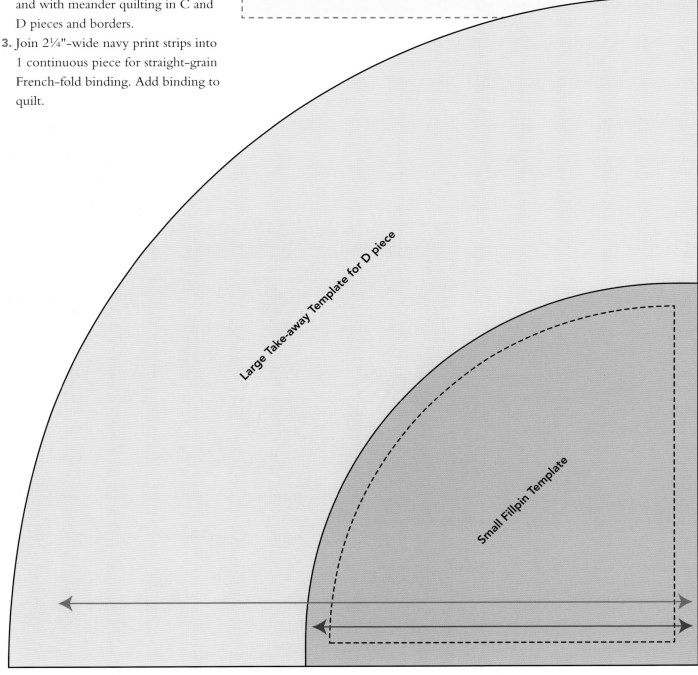

TRIED & TRUE

Tan paisley fabric adds interest to the large background pieces in this version of *New York Beauty*. To emphasize the arc points, choose fabrics that contrast strongly, such as the deep pink and green shown. Fabrics are from the "Three Sisters" collection by Moda™.

Large Take-away Template for D piece

Small Fillpin Template

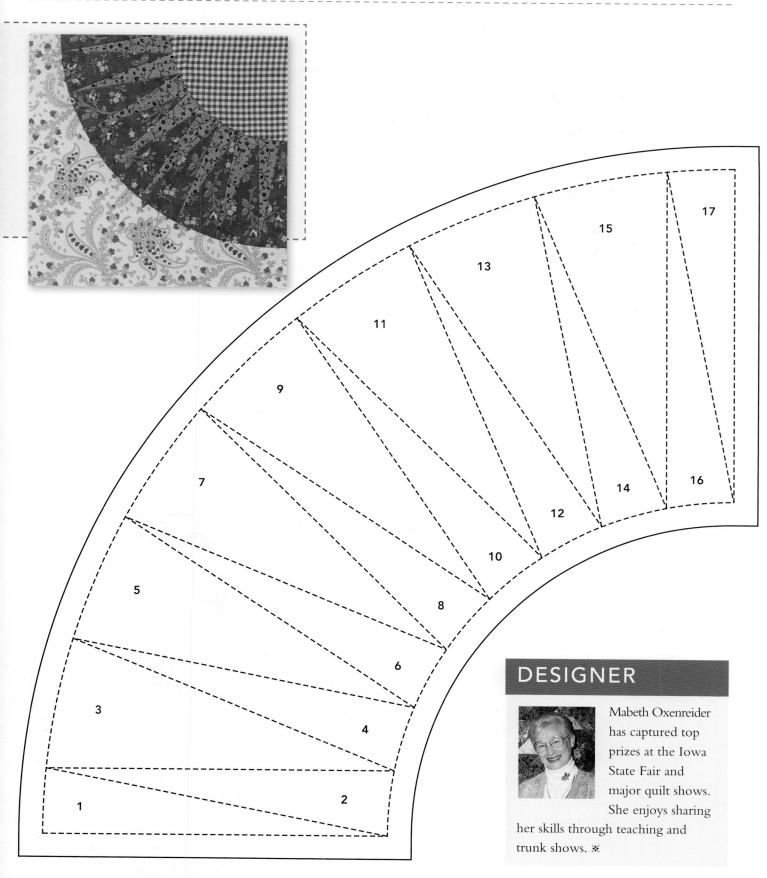

Arc Foundation Pattern

DESIGNER

Mabeth Oxenreider has captured top prizes at the Iowa State Fair and major quilt shows. She enjoys sharing her skills through teaching and trunk shows. ✳

New York Minute

Inspired by *New York Beauty,* Rebecca Brown used foundation piecing to make the long, tapered points sharp and accurate. High-contrast fabrics accentuate the crisp detail created by the slender points.

PROJECT RATING: CHALLENGING
Size: 21" × 21"
Blocks:
16 (4") New York Beauty blocks

MATERIALS

16 fat eighths★ assorted navy,
purple, gold, rust, and cream print
batiks for blocks
⅛ yard yellow print for inner
border
½ yard navy-and-yellow print for
outer border and binding
¾ yard backing fabric
27" square quilt batting
New York Minute Printed
Foundation Sheets or tracing
paper
Template material
Freezer paper
★fat eighth = 9" × 20"

Cutting

Make template for C and trace Take-
Away Template (shown in yellow) on
freezer paper. Patterns are on page 45.
Measurements include ¼" seam
allowances.

From each fat eighth, cut:
• 1 (4½") D square.
• 1 C piece.
• 9 (1¼" × 2½") rectangles for arc
background A pieces.
• 8 (1" × 2½") rectangles for B arc
points.

From yellow print, cut:
• 4 (1"-wide) strips for inner border.

From navy-and-yellow print, cut:
• 4 (2½"-wide) strips for outer border.
• 3 (2¼"-wide) strips for binding.

Block Assembly

Following instructions in *Sew Easy:
Piecing New York Beauty Blocks* on
pages 44–45, make 16 blocks (*Block
Diagram*). Use assorted fabrics for each
block.

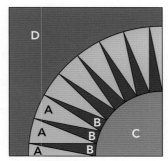

Block Diagram

Quilt Assembly

1. Referring to *Quilt Top Assembly
Diagram*, lay out blocks as shown.
2. Join blocks into rows; join rows to
complete quilt center.

3. Join 1 (1"-wide) yellow print strip to
1 (2½"-wide) navy-and-yellow print
strip as shown in *Strip Set Diagram*.
Make 4 strip sets.

Strip Set Diagram

4. Add border strip sets to quilt, mitering
corners.

Finishing

1. Layer backing, batting, and quilt top;
baste. Quilt as desired. Quilt shown
was machine quilted in the ditch in
the arcs and with meandering lines in
background and border.
2. Join 2¼"-wide navy-and-yellow
print strips into 1 continuous piece
for straight-grain French-fold binding.
Add binding to quilt. ✳

Quilt Top Assembly Diagram

Piecing New York Beauty Blocks

Long, tapered points like those in New York Beauty blocks can be difficult to work with using traditional patchwork methods. Foundation piecing simplifies this task and assures accuracy and sharp points.

Piecing the Arcs

1. Place background fabric (A) and point fabric (B) right sides together with wrong side of background fabric against un-marked side of foundation. Fabric edges should extend about ¼" beyond first sewing line as shown in *Photo A*.

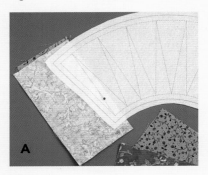

2. Using a short machine stitch, sew along first seam line, extending stitching into seam allowance at beginning and end of seam (*Photo B*).

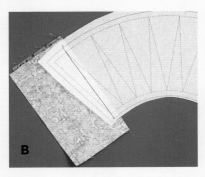

3. Turn foundation over, open out B fabric piece, and press (*Photo C*).

4. Fold foundation on stitching line; trim point B fabric ¼" beyond stitching (*Photo D*).

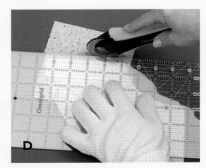

5. Open out fabrics to cover foundation. Place background fabric A piece right sides together with point fabric B and stitch along second diagonal line (*Photo E*).

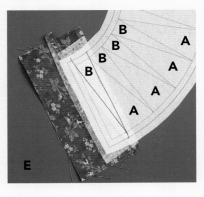

6. Open out background fabric A piece (*Photo F*). Press and trim as described in Step #4.

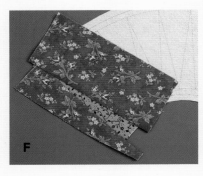

7. Continue in this manner until entire foundation is covered with fabric (*Photo G*).

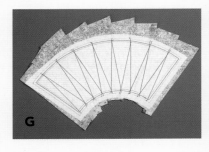

8. Trim excess fabric along outer line of foundation (*Photo H*).

Completing the Block

1. Use template to cut quarter-circle C piece.

2. To cut background D piece, begin with a 4½" fabric square. Align shiny side of freezer paper take-away template with corner of fabric square. Press lightly to adhere template to fabric. Cut along curved edge of template as shown in *Photo I*.

3. Remove freezer paper and discard quarter-circle fabric piece. Remaining portion of fabric square is piece D.

4. Lay out pieces for a block. Fold all pieces in half and mark center of curves by cutting a small notch as shown in *Photo J*.

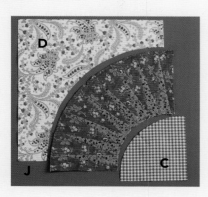

5. Matching centers of curves, join small quarter-circle C piece to inner edge of arc, stitching with arc on top.

6. Working with D piece on top, center and sew D piece to top edge of arc to complete block.

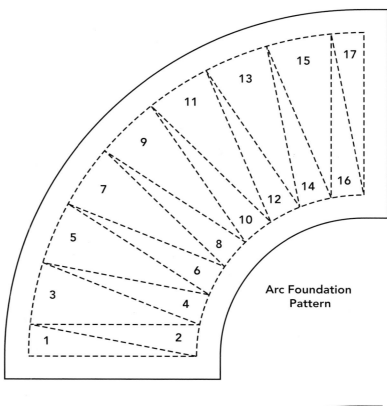

Arc Foundation Pattern

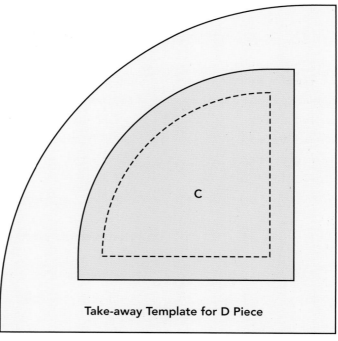

Take-away Template for D Piece

Chinese Fans

We're pleased to feature this great quilt from the International Quilt Study Center & Museum in Lincoln, Nebraska. The quiltmaker hand pieced her quilt, but we've provided a foundation pattern to make this project easier and quicker.

PROJECT RATING: CHALLENGING

Size: 87¾" × 87¾"

Blocks: 9 (24") Fan blocks

MATERIALS

20 fat quarters★ assorted 1930s prints for blocks

8¼ yards cream solid for background

1¼ yards lavender print

3½ yards purple solid for sashing, border, and binding

8¼ yards backing fabric

Queen-size quilt batting

★fat quarter = 18" × 20"

Cutting

Measurements include ¼" seam allowances. Patterns for templates and Arc Unit foundation are on pages 50–51. For instructions on paper foundation piecing, see *Sew Easy: Paper Foundation Piecing* on page 37.

From each 1930s print fat quarter, cut:

• 5 (3½"-wide) strips. From strips, cut 58 (3½" × 1½") rectangles.

From cream solid, cut:

• 1 (3½"-wide) strip. From strip, cut 4 (3½") sashing squares.

• 32 (3"-wide) strips. From each strip, cut 32 (3" × 1¼") rectangles.

• 144 B.

• 104 C.

From lavender print, cut:

• 144 A.

From purple solid, cut:

• 12 (3½"-wide) strips. From strips, cut 12 (3½" × 24½") sashing rectangles.

• 2¼"-wide bias strips to make about 475" of bias for binding.

• 112 D.

Block Assembly

1. Trace or photocopy 144 Arc Unit foundations.

2. Foundation piece Arc Units in numerical order, using assorted print rectangles for odd numbered sections and cream solid rectangles for even numbered sections. Make 144 Arc Units (*Arc Unit Diagram*).

Arc Unit Diagram

3. Lay out 1 Arc Unit, 1 lavender print A, and 1 cream solid B as shown in *Fan Unit Assembly Diagram*. Join to complete 1 Fan Unit (*Fan Unit Diagram*). Make 144 Fan Units.

Fan Unit Assembly Diagram

Fan Unit Diagram

QUILT FROM THE COLLECTION OF **International Quilt Study Center & Museum** 1997.007.0366.

Web **Extra**

For instructions on Sewing Curved
Seams visit our Web site at
www.FonsandPorter.com/secsp.

4. Lay out 16 Fan Units as shown in *Block Assembly Diagram*. Join into rows; join rows to complete 1 block *(Block Diagram)*. Make 9 blocks.

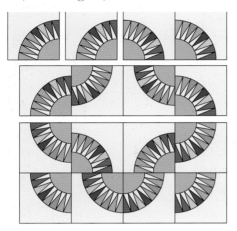

Block Assembly Diagram

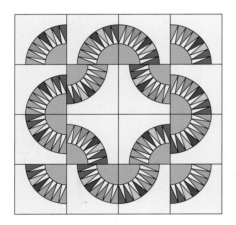

Block Diagram

Border Assembly

1. Join 27 purple solid D and 26 cream solid C as shown in *Quilt Top Assembly Diagram* to complete 1 side border. Make 2 side borders.

2. In a similar manner, join 29 purple solid D and 26 cream solid C to make top border. Repeat for bottom border.

Quilt Assembly

1. Lay out blocks, purple solid sashing rectangles, and cream solid sashing squares as shown in *Quilt Top Assembly Diagram*. Join into rows; join rows to complete quilt center.

2. Add side borders to sides of quilt center. Add top and bottom borders to quilt. Stitch seam between corner D pieces.

Finishing

1. Divide backing into 3 (2¾-yard) lengths. Join panels lengthwise.

2. Layer backing, batting, and quilt top; baste. Quilt as desired. Quilt shown was quilted with cross-hatching and feathers in blocks and outline quilting in border *(Quilting Diagra)*.

3. Add binding to quilt.

Quilting Diagram

Web **Extra**

For instructions on Binding Inside Corners for this project visit our Web site at www.FonsandPorter.com/sebic.

Quilt Top Assembly Diagram

ALTERNATE LAYOUT SUGGESTIONS

TRIED & TRUE

Darker reproduction fabrics by Jo Morton for Andover create another traditional look in this block.

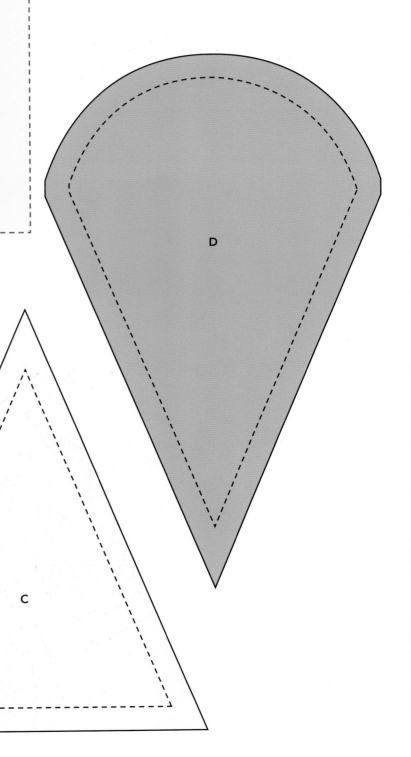

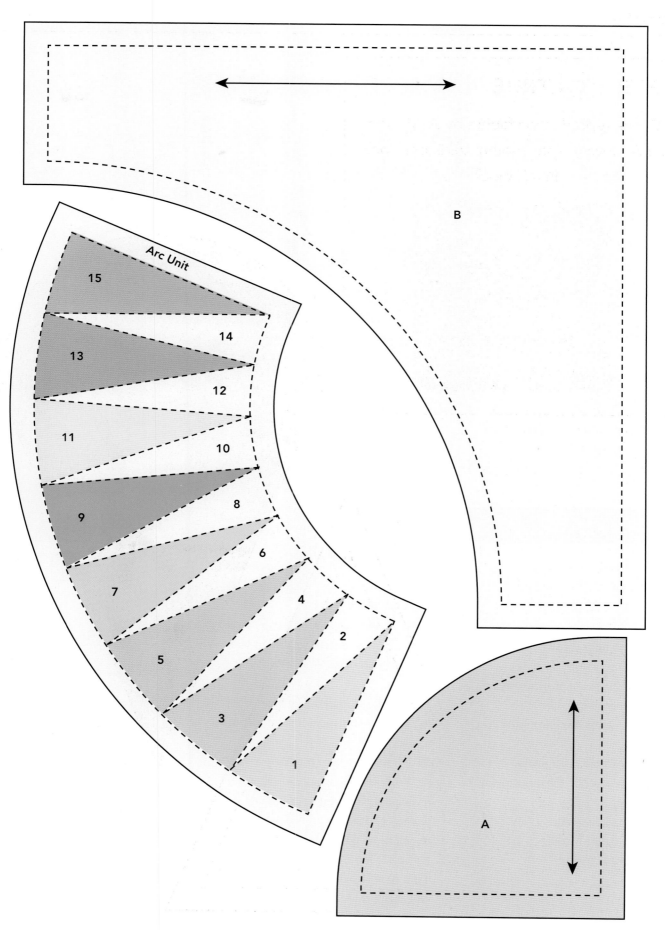

B

Arc Unit

15

14

13

12

11

10

9

8

7

6

5

4

3

2

1

A

Grandmother's Daisy Garden

Jodie Davis turned tricky piecing into paper foundation
piecing for her quilt. You can even piece the curved leaves on foundations!
See *Sew Easy: Paper Foundation Piecing* on page 58.

PROJECT RATING: INTERMEDIATE

Size: 54" × 78½"

Blocks: 12 (10" × 14⅝") Flower blocks

MATERIALS

4¼ yards blue print for blocks, outer border, and binding

1¾ yards cream print for blocks

⅜ yard gold print for blocks

¾ yard medium green print for blocks

¾ yard light green print for sashing and inner border

1½ yards green stripe for inner border

Paper for foundation piecing

Fons & Porter 60° Pyramids ruler (Optional)

3½ yards backing fabric

Twin-size quilt batting

Cutting

Measurements include ¼" seam allowances. Border strips are exact length needed. You may want to make them longer to allow for piecing variations. Patterns for foundation piecing are on pages 54–57.

NOTE: Pieces for foundation piecing are cut over-sized.

From blue print, cut:

• 2 (6½"-wide) strips. From strips, cut 12 (6½") squares. Cut squares in half diagonally to make 24 half-square F triangles.

• 5 (6"-wide) strips. From strips, cut 24 (6" × 7") D rectangles for foundation piecing.

• 18 (3"-wide) strips. From strips, cut 48 (3" × 6") rectangles and 96 (3" × 4") rectangles. Referring to *Trapezoid Cutting Diagrams*, trim ends of 3" × 6" rectangles on 60° angle to make 24 B trapezoids and 24 B reversed trapezoids. Trim 3" × 4" rectangles to make 48 C trapezoids and 48 C reversed trapezoids for foundation piecing.

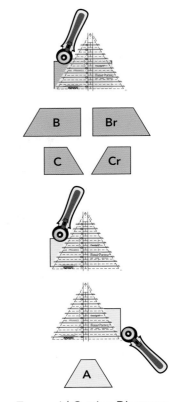

Trapezoid Cutting Diagrams

Sew **Smart**™

Use the Fons & Porter 60° Pyramids ruler to cut angles on trapezoids A, B, and C. —Jodie

- 7 (2½"-wide) strips. Piece strips to make 2 (2½" × 75") side outer borders and 2 (2½" × 54½") top and bottom outer borders.
- 8 (2¼"-wide) strips for binding.
- 4 (1⅞"-wide) strips. From strips, cut 12 (1⅞" × 10½") H rectangles.

From cream print, cut:
- 18 (3"-wide) strips. From strips, cut 144 (3" × 5") rectangles. Referring to *Trapezoid Cutting Diagrams*, trim rectangles to make 144 A trapezoids for foundation piecing.

From gold print, cut:
- 3 (3"-wide) strips. From strips, cut 24 (3" × 5") rectangles. Referring to *Trapezoid Cutting Diagrams*, trim rectangles to make 24 A trapezoids for foundation piecing.

From medium green print, cut:
- 3 (7"-wide) strips. From strips, cut 24 (7" × 5") E rectangles for foundation piecing.
- 2 (1"-wide) strips. From strips, cut 12 (1" × 5½") G rectangles.

From light green print, cut:
- 9 (2½"-wide) strips. From 2 strips, cut 2 (2½" × 38½") top and bottom inner borders. Piece remaining strips to make 4 (2½" × 59") sashing strips.

From green stripe, cut:
- 7 (6½"-wide) strips. Piece strips to make 2 (6½" × 63") side middle borders and 2 (6½" × 50½") top and bottom middle borders.

  NOTE: For instructions on paper piecing, see *Sew Easy: Paper Foundation Piecing* on page 58 and *Sew Easy: Paper Foundation Piecing Curves* on page 59.

Flower Unit Assembly

1. Trace or photocopy 12 Flower Segment 1, 12 Flower Segment 2, and 12 Flower Segment 3.

2. Foundation piece Flower Segments in numerical order, using trapezoid pieces A, B, and C as indicated. For detailed instructions, see *Sew Easy: Paper Foundation Piecing* on page 58.

3. Lay out 2 Flower Segment 1, 2 Flower Segment 2, and 2 Flower Segment 3 as shown in *Flower Unit Diagram*. Join segments to complete 1 Flower Unit. Make 12 Flower Units.

Leaf Unit Assembly

1. Trace or photocopy 12 Leaf Segments and 12 Leaf Segments reversed.

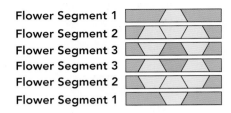

Flower Segment 1	
Flower Segment 2	
Flower Segment 3	
Flower Segment 3	
Flower Segment 2	
Flower Segment 1	

Flower Unit Diagram

2. Referring to *Sew Easy: Paper Foundation Piecing Curves* on page 59, foundation piece Leaf Segments in numerical order, using pieces D, E, and F.

3. Join 1 Leaf Segment, 1 Leaf Segment reversed, and 1 medium green print G rectangle as shown in *Leaf Unit Diagrams*. Make 12 Leaf Units.

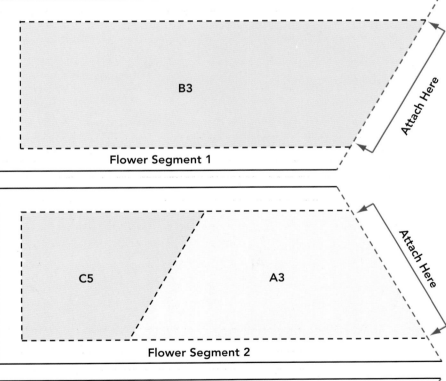

B3

Attach Here

Flower Segment 1

C5 A3

Attach Here

Flower Segment 2

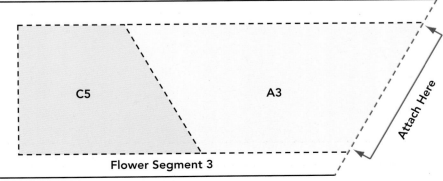

C5 A3

Attach Here

Flower Segment 3

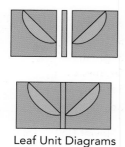

Leaf Unit Diagrams

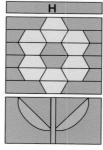

H

Block Assembly
Diagram

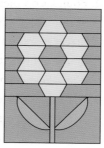

Block Diagram

Block Assembly

1. Lay out 1 blue print H rectangle, 1 Flower Unit, and 1 Leaf Unit as shown in *Block Assembly Diagram*. Join to complete 1 block (*Block Diagram*).
2. Make 12 blocks.

Quilt Assembly

1. Lay out blocks and sashing rectangles as shown in *Quilt Top Assembly Diagram* on page 56. Join blocks into vertical rows; join rows to complete quilt center.
2. Add light green top and bottom inner borders to quilt center.
3. Add green stripe side middle borders to quilt center. Add green stripe top and bottom middle borders to quilt.
4. Repeat for blue print outer borders.

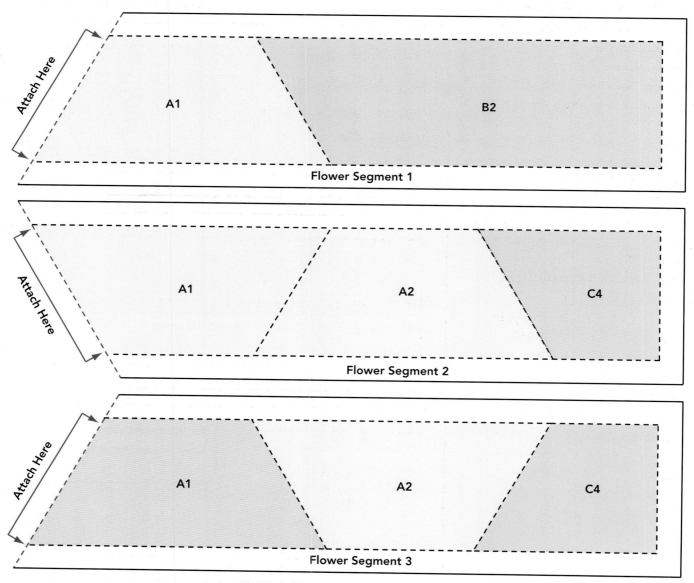

Attach Here

A1   B2

Flower Segment 1

Attach Here

A1   A2   C4

Flower Segment 2

Attach Here

A1   A2   C4

Flower Segment 3

Finishing

1. Divide backing into 2 (1¾-yard) lengths. Join panels lengthwise. Seam will run horizontally.

2. Layer backing, batting, and quilt top; baste. Quilt as desired. Quilt shown was quilted with a picket fence, watering cans, and garden gloves in middle and outer borders, and a leaf design in sashing and inner border. The blocks were outline quilted and have a Greek Key design in hexagons *(Quilting Diagram)*.

3. Join 2¼"-wide blue print strips into 1 continuous piece for straight-grain French-fold binding. Add binding to quilt.

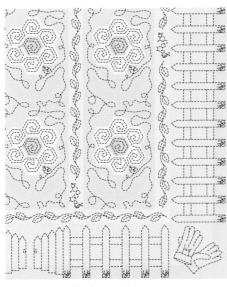

Quilting Diagram

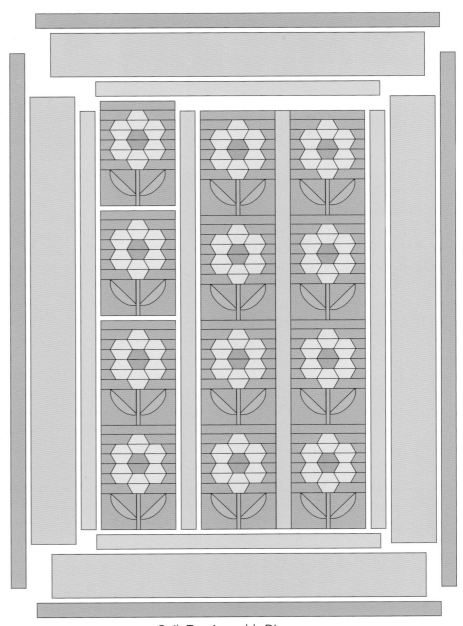

Quilt Top Assembly Diagram

DESIGNER

Jodie Davis loves paper piecing. The idea for this project came to her in the middle of the night. She tried it, and it worked! Now she loves to share curved paper piecing with other quilters. Watch Jodie on QNNtv.com in "Quilt Out Loud" and "Quilt It! The Longarm Quilting Show."

Web **Extra**

To download full size quilting designs for this project visit our Web site at www.FonsandPorter.com/gdgdesigns.

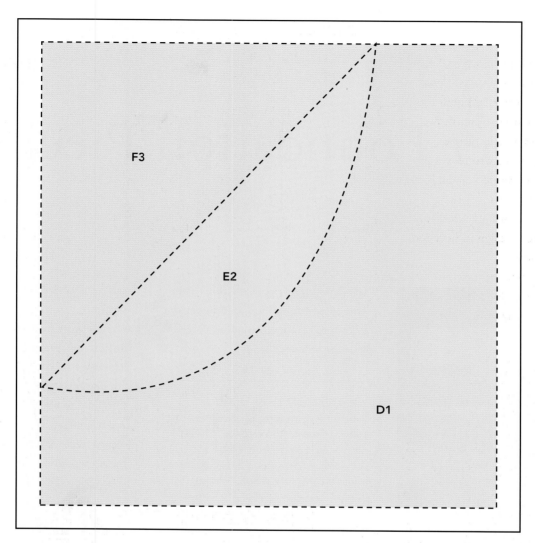

F3

E2

D1

Leaf Segment

TRIED & TRUE

Use a variety of batiks as we did to make this lively version of the Grandmother's Daisy block. Fabrics are from Timeless Treasures and Moda. ✳

Paper Foundation Piecing

Paper Foundation piecing is ideal for designs with odd angles and sizes of pieces. Use this method for the Flower Segments in *Grandmother's Daisy Garden* on page 52.

A

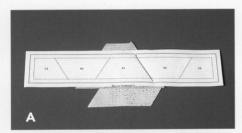

B

C

1. Using ruler and pencil, trace all lines and outer edge of foundation pattern onto tracing paper. Number pieces to indicate stitching order.

Sew **Smart**™

Save time by making photocopies on special foundation papers. Check photocopied patterns to be sure they are correct size. (Some copiers may distort copy size.) —Liz

2. Using fabric pieces that are larger than the numbered areas, place fabrics for #1 and #2 right sides together. Position paper pattern atop fabrics with printed side of paper facing you (*Photo A*). Make sure the fabric for #1 is under that area and that edges of fabrics extend ¼" beyond stitching line between the two sections.

3. Using a short machine stitch so papers will tear off easily later, stitch on line between the two areas, extending stitching into seam allowances at ends of seams.

4. Open out pieces and press or finger press the seam (*Photo B*). The right sides of the fabric pieces will be facing

out on the back side of the paper pattern.

5. Flip the work over and fold back paper pattern on stitched line. Trim seam allowance to ¼", being careful not to cut paper pattern (*Photo C*).

6. Continue to add pieces in numerical order until pattern is covered. Use rotary cutter and ruler to trim excess paper and fabric along outer pattern lines (*Photo D*).

7. Make 2 each Flower Segments 1, 2, and 3 for each Flower Unit.

8. Carefully tear off foundation paper after blocks are joined.

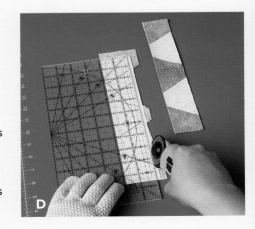

D

Paper Foundation Piecing Curves

Use this easy method to make textured, curved leaves for *Grandmother's Daisy Garden* on page 52.

1. Using ruler and pencil, trace all lines and outer edge of foundation pattern onto tracing paper. Number pieces to indicate stitching order.

> ### Sew Smart™
> Save time by making photocopies on special foundation papers. Check photocopied patterns to be sure they are correct size. (Some copiers may distort copy size.) —Liz

2. Using fabric pieces that are larger than the numbered areas, place fabrics for #1 and #2 right sides together. Position paper pattern atop fabrics with printed side of paper facing you *(Photo A)*. Make sure the fabric for #2 is under that area and extends ¼" beyond curved stitching line between the two sections and that edge of fabric for #1 extends ¼" beyond stitching line between sections #1 and #2.

> ### Sew Smart™
> Fabric piece #2 is much larger than you think you'll need. Pleats take up a lot of room. Make sure the extra fabric for #2 is in the "cup" of the curve. —Jodie

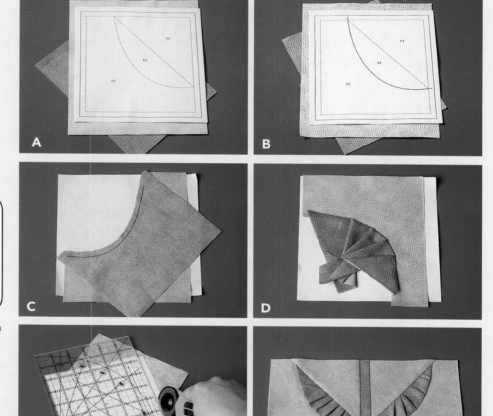

3. Using a short machine stitch so papers will tear off easily later, stitch on the curved line between the two areas, extending stitching into seam allowances at ends of seams *(Photo B)*. Trim seam allowance to ¼" *(Photo C)*.

4. Open out pieces and finger press pleats in piece #2 *(Photo D)*. Baste pleats in place.

5. Continue to add pieces in numerical order until pattern is covered. Use rotary cutter and ruler to trim excess paper and fabric along outer pattern lines *(Photo E)*.

6. Join pieced sections to complete Stem Unit *(Photo F)*.

7. Carefully tear off foundation paper after blocks are joined.

Flying Geese

This wonderful quilt from the collection of the International Quilt Study Center & Museum in Lincoln, Nebraska, was hand pieced by an unknown quiltmaker in the late 1800s. We've simplified the construction for you by providing foundation patterns for the geese units.

PROJECT RATING: CHALLENGING

Size: 75" × 75"

Blocks: 16 (18¾") Flying Geese blocks

MATERIALS

¾ yard each of 8 assorted blue prints

5½ yards cream solid for background

¾ yard blue stripe for binding

Paper for foundations

4½ yards backing fabric

Full-size quilt batting

Cutting

Measurements include ¼" seam allowances. Patterns for Diamond and Foundations are on pages 62–63. A and B triangles are oversized for foundation piecing.

From each blue print, cut:

• 6 (2½"-wide) strips. From strips, cut 96 (2½") squares. Cut squares in half diagonally to make 192 half-square B triangles.

• 2 sets of 8 matching Diamonds.

• 2 (4") squares. Cut squares in half diagonally in both directions to make 8 quarter-square A triangles.

From cream solid, cut:

• 13 (7¼"-wide) strips. From strips, cut 64 (7¼") squares. Cut squares in half diagonally to make 128 half-square C triangles.

• 23 (4"-wide) strips. From strips, cut 224 (4") squares. Cut squares in half diagonally in both directions to make 896 quarter-square A triangles.

From blue stripe, cut:

• 9 (2¼"-wide) strips for binding.

Block Assembly

1. Trace or photocopy 64 each of Foundations 1 and 2 onto paper. Roughly cut out patterns.

2. Referring to *Foundation Diagrams*, piece foundations in numerical order using assorted blue print B triangles, cream solid A triangles, and assorted blue print A triangles. Make 64 Foundation 1 and 64 Foundation 2.

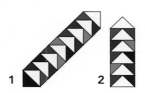

Foundation Diagrams

3. Add 2 cream C triangles to 1 Foundation 1 as shown in *Corner Unit Diagram*. Make 64 Corner Units.

Corner Unit Diagram

4. Choose 1 set of 8 matching Diamonds and 4 Foundation 2.

5. Stitch 2 Diamonds together, stopping and backstitching at the dot as shown in *Diamond Diagram*. Set 1 Foundation 2 into Diamonds as shown in *Center Unit Diagram*. Make 4 Center Units.

Diamond Diagram   **Center Unit Diagram**

6. Join 4 Center Units as shown in *Center Section Diagram*, backstitching at dots.

Center Section Diagram

7. Set 4 Corner Units into Center Section to complete 1 block *(Block Diagram)*. Make 16 blocks.

Block Diagram

Quilt Assembly

1. Lay out blocks as shown in *Quilt Top Assembly Diagram* on page 62.

2. Join blocks into rows; join rows to complete quilt top.

Finishing

1. Divide backing into 2 (2¼-yard) lengths. Cut 1 piece in half lengthwise to make 2 narrow panels. Join 1 narrow panel to each side of wider panel; press seam allowances toward narrow panels.

2. Layer backing, batting, and quilt top; baste. Quilt as desired.

3. Join 2¼"-wide blue stripe strips into 1 continuous piece for straight-grain French-fold binding. Add binding to quilt.

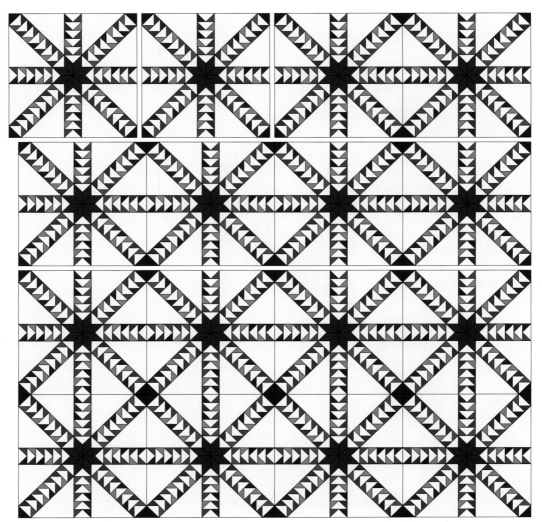

Quilt Top Assembly Diagram

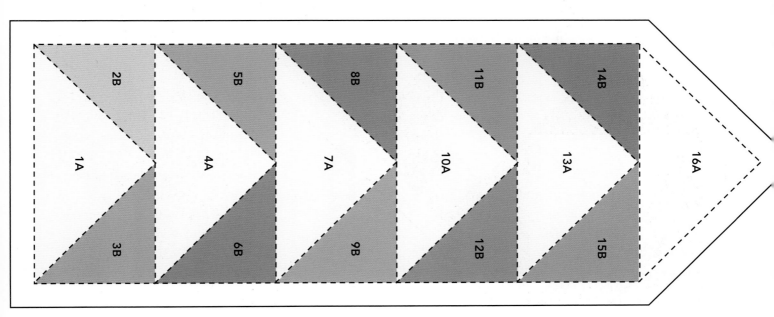

Foundation 2

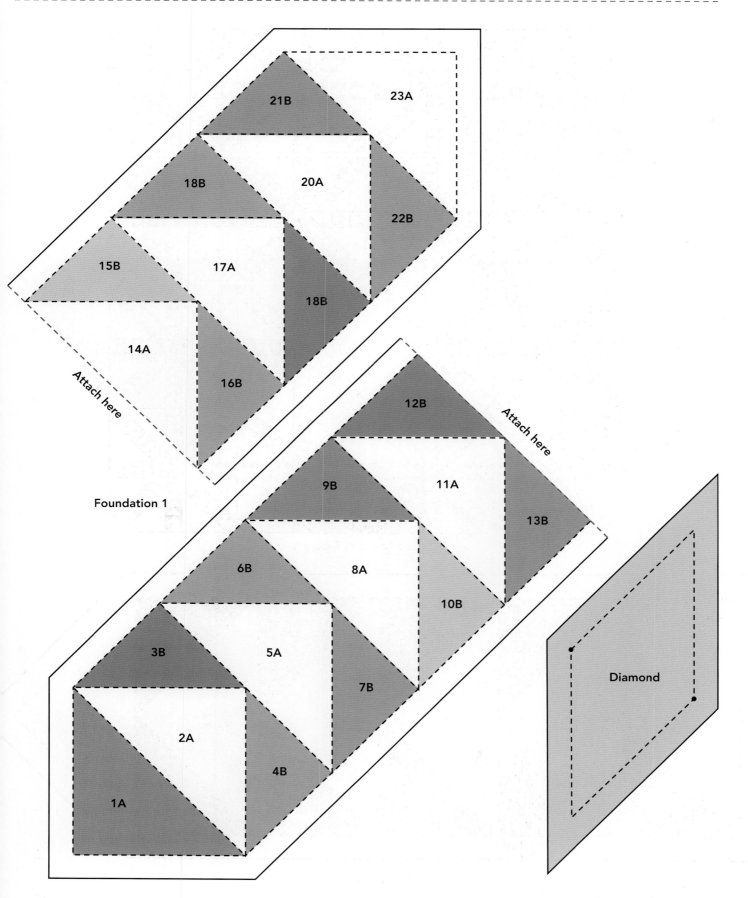

Foundation 1

Attach here

Diamond

Night Flight

Foundation paper piecing makes the flying geese units in this
quilt easy to stitch. Designer Shon McMain used gradations of hand-dyed fabrics
combined with solid black to create her miniature quilt.

PROJECT RATING: INTERMEDIATE
Size: 11½" × 15¼"

MATERIALS

1 (6") square each of 4 greens, 3 blues, 3 purples, and 3 pinks
½ yard black for background, border, and binding
Tracing paper
15" × 19" rectangle backing fabric
15" × 19" rectangle quilt batting

Cutting

Patterns for paper foundation piecing are on page 66. Measurements include ¼" seam allowances.

From black, cut:

• 2 (2"-wide) strips. From strips, cut 2 (2½" × 17") side borders and 2 (2½" × 13½") top and bottom borders. (Borders are over-sized and will be trimmed later.)
• 2 (2¼"-wide) strips for binding.

Row 1 Assembly

1. Using patterns on page 66, trace 2 Section A and 1 Section B. Referring to photo at right for color placement, stitch each section using paper foundation piecing. Trim each section on outer cutting lines.

2. Join 1 Section A to each end of Section B to complete Row 1. Make 3 of Row 1.

Row 2 Assembly

1. Using patterns on page 66, trace Section C and Section D. Referring to photo at right for color placement, stitch each section using paper foundation piecing. Trim each section on outer cutting lines.

2. Join Section C to top of Section D to complete Row 2. Make 2 of Row 2.

Quilt Assembly

1. Lay out rows as shown in photo and *Quilt Center Reference Diagram* on page 66. Join rows to complete quilt center.

2. Join borders to quilt, mitering corners. (See *Sew Easy: Mitered Borders* on page 67.)

Finishing

1. Layer backing, batting, and quilt top; baste. Quilt as desired. Quilt shown was quilted in the ditch around rows and with diagonal lines in the border.

2. Join 2¼"-wide black strips into 1 continuous piece for straight-grain French-fold binding. Add binding to quilt.

DESIGNER

Iowa quilter Shon McMain enjoys trying new techniques and working with many different types of fabric. Her quilts have often been featured in *Love of Quilting*. ✳

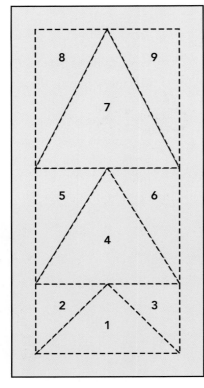

Section A

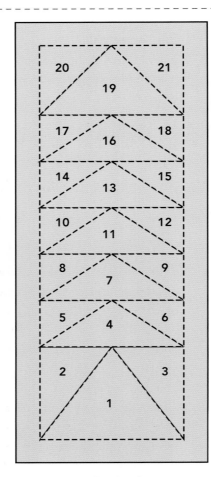

Section B

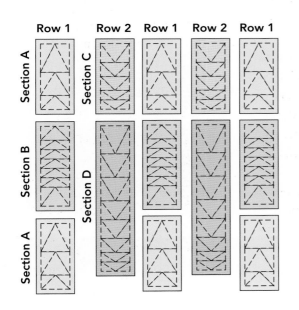

	Row 1	Row 2	Row 1	Row 2	Row 1
Section A					
Section C					
Section B					
Section D					
Section A					

Quilt Center Reference Diagram

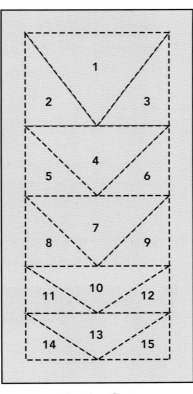

Section C

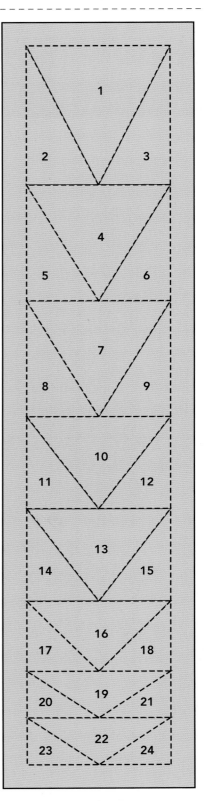

Section D

Mitered Borders

The subtle seam of a mitered corner creates the illusion of a continuous line around the quilt. Mitered corners are ideal for striped fabric borders or multiple plain borders.

1. Referring to *Measuring Diagram*, measure your quilt length through the middle of the quilt rather than along the edges. In the same manner, measure quilt width. Add to your measurements twice the planned width of the border plus 2". Trim borders to these measurements.

Measuring Diagram

2. On wrong side of quilt top, mark ¼" seam allowances at each corner.

3. Fold quilt top in half and place a pin at the center of the quilt side. Fold border in half and mark center with pin.

4. With right sides facing and raw edges aligned, match center pins on the border and the quilt. Working from the center out, pin the border to the quilt, right sides facing. The border will extend beyond the quilt edges. Do not trim the border.

5. Sew the border to the quilt. Start and stop stitching ¼" from the corner of the quilt top, backstitching at each end. Press the seam allowance toward the border. Add the remaining borders in the same manner.

6. With right sides facing, fold the quilt diagonally as shown in *Mitering Diagram 1*, aligning the raw edges of the adjacent borders. Pin securely.

7. Align a ruler along the diagonal fold, as shown in *Mitering Diagram 2*. Holding the ruler firmly, mark a line from the end of the border seam to the raw edge.

8. Start machine stitching at the beginning of the marked line, backstitch, and then stitch on the line out to the raw edge.

9. Unfold the quilt to be sure that the corner lies flat (*Mitered Borders Diagram*). Correct the stitching if necessary. Trim the seam allowance to ¼".

10. Miter the remaining corners. Press the corner seams open.

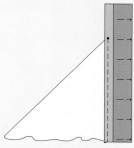

Mitering Diagram 1

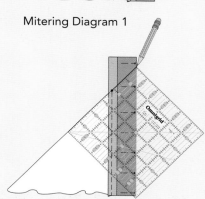

Mitering Diagram 2

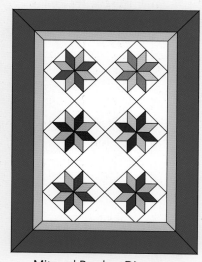

Mitered Borders Diagram

Northern Lights

A single, dramatic, multicolored stripe fabric designed by Caryl Bryer Fallert for Benartex® was used for the borders, setting pieces, and patchwork stars of this dramatic quilt. By "fussy cutting" the various pieces for the quilt from different areas of the fabric, maker Lynn Witzenburg created a project that appears to be made of many fabrics.

PROJECT RATING: INTERMEDIATE
Size: 20⅝" × 20⅝"
Blocks: 9 (2¾") Star blocks

MATERIALS

¾ yard multicolored fabric for stars, setting pieces, and borders
¼ yard yellow print for block backgrounds and border
½ yard black print for block sashing, inner border, and binding
Tracing paper
¾ yard backing fabric
25" square of quilt batting

Cutting

Pattern for paper foundation piecing star point units at right. Measurements include ¼" seam allowances.

From multicolored fabric, cut:
• 4 (4¼"-wide) outer border strips.
• 2 (5⅛") squares. Cut squares in half diagonally in both directions to make 8 quarter-square side setting triangles. You may want to cut extras to get desired colors for triangles.
• 4 (3¼") setting squares.
• 2 (2⅞") squares. Cut squares in half diagonally to make 4 half-square corner setting triangles.
• 9 (1¼") A squares for stars.
• 72 (1" × 1½") rectangles for star points.

From yellow print, cut:
• 3 (1¼"-wide) strips. From strips, cut 72 (1¼") A squares for block corners and #1 pieces.
• 2 (¾"-wide) strips. From strips, cut 4 (¾" × 12⅛") border strips.

From black print, cut:
• 3 (¾"-wide) strips. From strips, cut 18 (¾" × 2¾") B sashing strips and 18 (¾" × 3¼") C sashing strips.
• 2 (1¼"-wide) strips. From strips, cut 2 (1¼" × 12⅛") side inner borders and 2 (1¼" × 13⅝") top and bottom inner borders.
• 3 (2¼"-wide) strips for binding.

Block Assembly

1. Trace *Star Point Unit Paper Piecing Pattern* 4 times to make 1 block. Choose 1 yellow A square for piece #1 and 2 multicolor star point rectangles for pieces #2 and #3. Join pieces using paper foundation piecing. Trim unit and remove paper to complete star point unit. Make 4 star point units.

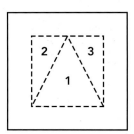

Star Point Unit Paper Piecing Pattern

2. Referring to *Block Assembly Diagram*, lay out 4 star point units, 1 multicolor A square, and 4 yellow A squares. Join into horizontal rows; join rows.

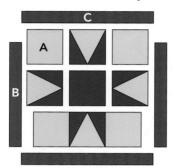

Block Assembly Diagram

3. Add 1 B sashing strip to each side. Add C sashing strips to top and bottom to complete 1 Star block *(Block Diagram)*. Make 9 blocks.

Block Diagram

Quilt Assembly

1. Referring to photo on page 68, lay out blocks, setting squares and setting triangles. Join into diagonal rows; join rows to complete quilt center.

2. Press yellow border strips in half lengthwise. Align raw edges of folded strip with 1 side of quilt; pin in place. Repeat for remaining sides.

> **Sew Smart™**
> Adding a narrow flange like this is a slick way to create what appears to be a very narrow border.
> —Marianne

3. Attach 1 black print side inner border to side of quilt. Press seam toward border. Repeat for opposite side. Attach top and bottom inner borders to quilt.

4. Attach multicolor outer borders to quilt, mitering corners. (See *Sew Easy: Mitered Borders* on page 67.)

Finishing

1. Layer backing, batting, and quilt top; baste. Quilt as desired. Quilt shown was quilted in the ditch around stars and blocks and with feather designs (see page 71) in the setting pieces and outer border.

2. Join 2¼"-wide black print strips into 1 continuous piece for straight-grain French-fold binding. Add binding to quilt.

Try **This!**

Look for fabric similar to this one ("Glacier Park" by Caryl Bryer Fallert for Benartex) to make your mini quilt. By "fussy cutting," you can get several colors of stars and setting pieces from one piece of fabric.

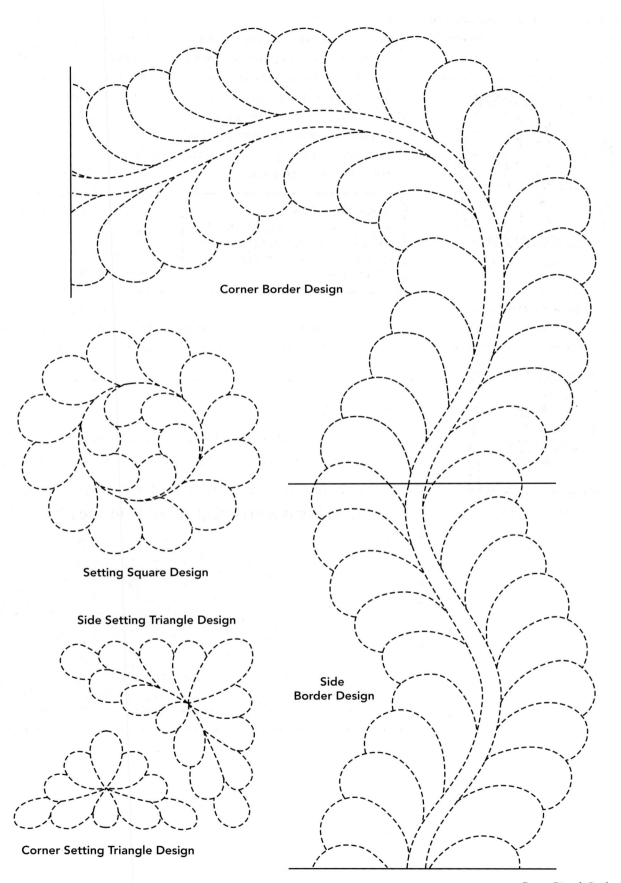

Corner Border Design

Setting Square Design

Side Setting Triangle Design

Side
Border Design

Corner Setting Triangle Design

Summer Heat

Designer Nancy Mahoney made creating sharp points and unusual angles easy with foundation piecing. Aptly named, this quilt seems to radiate heat.

PROJECT RATING: INTERMEDIATE

Size: 64" × 64"

Blocks: 16 (12") blocks

MATERIALS

1 yard yellow print for blocks

2¼ yards black dot print for blocks

1¾ yards red dot print for blocks and inner border

1⅜ yards yellow dot print for blocks

1⅛ yards red stripe for blocks and binding

1 yard black-and-white print #1 for blocks

1 yard black-and-white print #2 for outer border

¾ yard black print for sashing

Paper for foundation piecing

4 yards backing fabric

Twin-size quilt batting

Cutting

Measurements include ¼" seam allowances. Border strips are exact length needed. You may want to make them longer to allow for piecing variations. Patterns for foundations are on pages 76 and 77. For instructions on paper piecing, see *Sew Easy: Paper Foundation Piecing* on page 37. Pieces are cut over-size for foundation piecing.

From yellow print, cut:

• 5 (2¾"-wide) strips. From strips, cut 64 (2¾") squares for A8.

• 12 (1½"-wide) strips. From strips, cut 128 (1½" × 3½") rectangles for A6 and A7.

From black dot print, cut:

• 8 (2¾"-wide) strips. From strips, cut 64 (2¾" × 4¼") rectangles for A5.

• 8 (2½"-wide) strips. From strips, cut 64 (2½" × 5") rectangles for B1.

• 15 (2"-wide) strips. From strips, cut 128 (2" × 4¼") rectangles for A3 and A4.

From red dot print, cut:

• 20 (2¼"-wide) strips. From strips, cut 256 (2¼" × 3") rectangles for B2, B3, C2, and C3.

• 6 (2"-wide) strips. Piece strips to make 2 (2" × 56½") top and bottom inner borders and 2 (2" × 53½") side inner borders.

From yellow dot print, cut:

• 5 (3"-wide) strips. From strips, cut 64 (3") squares for C1.

• 10 (2"-wide) strips. From strips, cut 128 (2" × 3") rectangles for C4 and C5.

• 6 (1¾"-wide) strips. From strips, cut 64 (1¾" × 3½") rectangles for A2.

From red stripe, cut:

• 7 (2¼"-wide) strips for binding.

• 11 (1¾"-wide) strips. From strips, cut 64 (1¾" × 6") rectangles for A1.

From black-and-white print #1, cut:

• 5 (5½"-wide) strips. From strips, cut 32 (5½") squares. Cut squares in half diagonally to make 64 half-square triangles for C6.

From black-and-white print #2, cut:

- 7 (4½"-wide) strips. Piece strips to make 2 (4½" × 64½") top and bottom outer borders and 2 (4½" × 56½") side outer borders.

From black print, cut:

- 14 (1½"-wide) strips. From strips, cut 12 (1½" × 12½") D sashing rectangles. Piece remaining strips to make 2 (1½" × 53½") F sashing rectangles and 5 (1½" × 51½") E sashing rectangles.

Block Assembly

1. Trace or photocopy 64 each of Foundation Units A, B, and C.
2. Referring to *Foundation Diagrams*, paper piece foundation units in numerical order. Make 64 each Units A, B, and C.

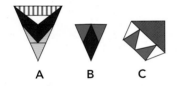

A   B   C

Foundation Diagrams

3. Join 1 Unit B and 1 Unit C as shown in *Corner Unit Diagram*. Make 64 Corner Units.

Corner Unit Diagram

4. Lay out 4 Unit A and 4 Corner Units as shown in *Block Assembly Diagram*. Join to complete 1 block *(Block Diagram)*. Make 16 blocks.

Block Assembly Diagram

Block Diagram

Quilt Assembly

1. Lay out blocks and D and E sashing rectangles as shown in *Quilt Top Assembly Diagram*. Join into rows; join rows. Add F sashing rectangles to sides to complete quilt center.
2. Add red dot print side inner borders to quilt center. Add top and bottom inner borders to quilt.
3. Repeat for black-and-white print #2 outer borders.

Finishing

1. Divide backing into 2 (2-yard) lengths. Cut 1 piece in half lengthwise to make 2 narrow panels. Join 1 narrow panel to each side of wider panel; press seam allowances toward narrow panels.
2. Layer backing, batting, and quilt top; baste. Quilt as desired. Quilt shown was quilted in the ditch and with a flower design in outer border *(Quilting Diagram* on page 75).

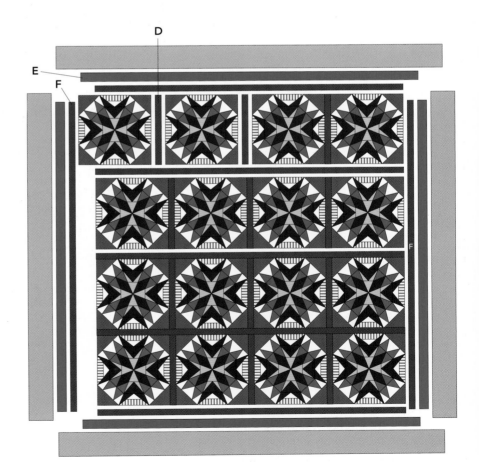

Quilt Top Assembly Diagram

3. Join 2¼"-wide red stripe strips into 1 continuous piece for straight-grain French-fold binding. Add binding to quilt.

Quilting Diagram

DESIGNER

Designer Nancy Mahoney is a quilting teacher, fabric designer, and author of ten books. She enjoys making traditional quilts using new techniques that make quiltmaking easy and fun. Look for her book, *Treasures from the '30s*, published by Martingale & Company. ✳

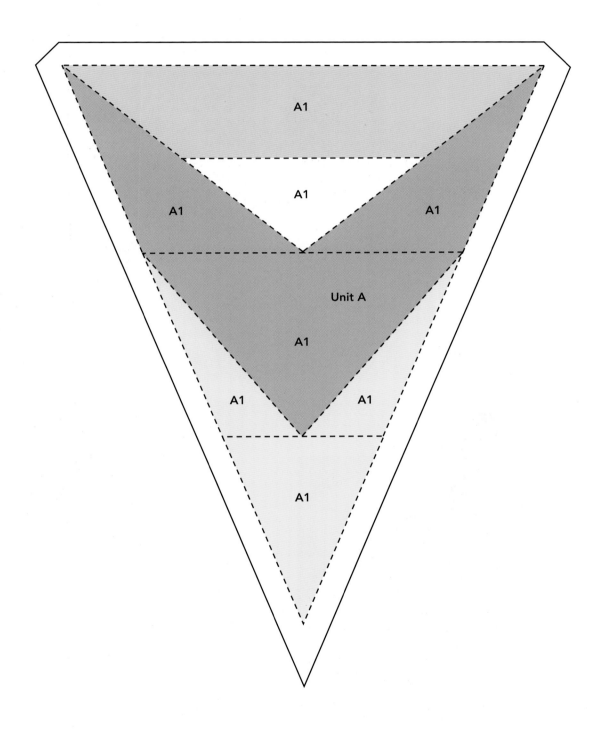

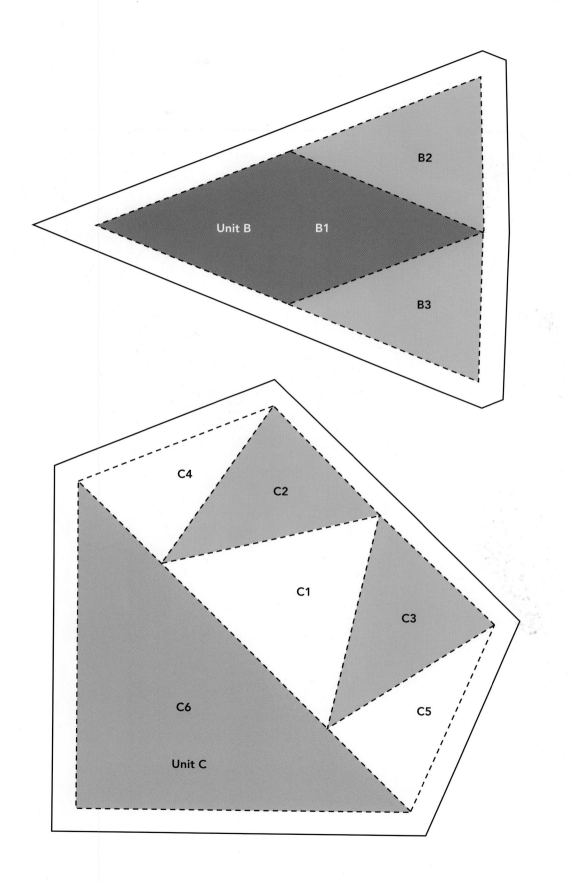

Star Rosettes

Nancy Mahoney used red and black prints to provide perfect contrast with the white print background in her quilt. The blocks are easily pieced on paper foundations.

PROJECT RATING: INTERMEDIATE
Size: 58" × 70"
Blocks: 20 (12") Star blocks

MATERIALS

1⅜ yards red print
1 yard red stripe
1 yard red check
¾ yard black print for blocks
1¾ yards black floral for border and
   binding
1⅜ yards red-on-white print
3⅛ yards black-on-white print
Paper for foundations
3½ yards backing fabric
Twin-size quilt batting

Cutting

Measurements include ¼" seam allowances. Border strips are exact length needed. You may want to make them longer to allow for piecing variations. Foundation patterns are on page 81. For instructions on paper foundation piecing, see *Sew Easy: Paper Foundation Piecing* on page 37.

From red print, cut:
• 8 (5½"-wide) strips. From strips, cut 80 (5½" × 4") A1 rectangles.

From red stripe, cut:
• 10 (3"-wide) strips. From strips, cut 80 (3" × 5") B1 rectangles.

From red check, cut:
• 7 (4½"-wide) strips. From strips, cut 80 (4½" × 3") B4 rectangles.

From black print, cut:
• 8 (3"-wide) strips. From strips, cut 80 (3" × 4") A4 rectangles.

From black floral, cut:
• 4 (5½"-wide) **lengthwise** strips. From strips, cut 2 (5½" × 60½") side borders and 2 (5½" × 58½") top and bottom borders.
• 5 (2¼"-wide) **lengthwise** strips for binding.

From red-on-white print, cut:
• 15 (3"-wide) strips. From strips, cut a total of 240 (3" × 2½") rectangles (A5, B2, B3).

From black-on-white print, cut:
• 10 (6"-wide) strips. From strips, cut a total of 160 (6" × 2½") rectangles (A2, A3).
• 13 (3½"-wide) strips. From strips, cut a total of 160 (3½" × 3") rectangles (B5, B6).

Block Assembly

1. Trace or photocopy 80 each of Foundation A and B.

2. Referring to *Foundation Diagrams*, paper piece foundations in numerical order. Make 80 Foundation A and 80 Foundation B.

A   **B**
Foundation Diagrams

3. Lay out 4 Foundation A and 4 Foundation B as shown in *Block Assembly Diagrams* on page 80. Join to complete 1 block *(Block Diagram)*. Make 20 blocks.

Quilt Assembly

1. Lay out blocks as shown in *Quilt Top Assembly Diagram* on page 80. Join into rows; join rows to complete quilt center.

2. Add side borders to quilt center. Add top and bottom borders to quilt.

Block Assembly Diagrams

Block Diagram

Finishing

1. Divide backing into 2 (1¾-yard) lengths. Join panels lengthwise. Seam will run horizontally.

2. Layer backing, batting, and quilt top; baste. Quilt as desired. Quilt shown was quilted with a leaf design in the blocks, and with overlapping hearts in the border *(Quilting Diagram)*.

3. Join 2¼"-wide black floral strips into 1 continuous piece for straight-grain French-fold binding. Add binding to quilt.

Quilting Diagram

Quilt Top Assembly Diagram

TRIED & TRUE

These trendy pink and aqua prints from Have a Sheri Berry Holiday by Lyndhurst Studio are pretty any time of year.

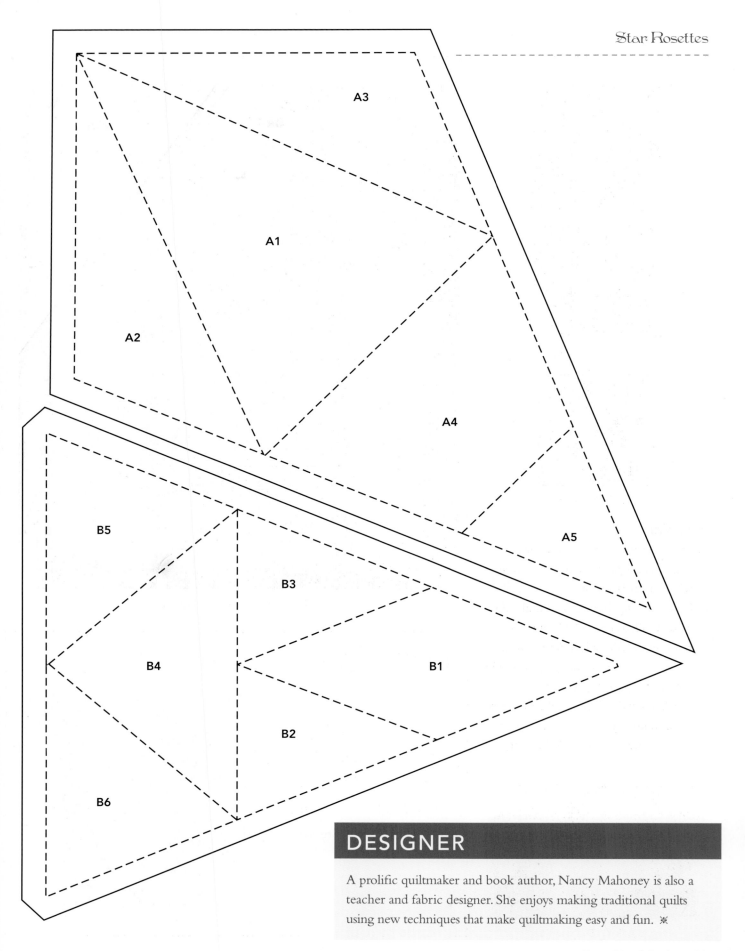

A3

A1

A2

A4

A5

B5

B3

B4

B1

B2

B6

DESIGNER

A prolific quiltmaker and book author, Nancy Mahoney is also a teacher and fabric designer. She enjoys making traditional quilts using new techniques that make quiltmaking easy and fun. ✳

Windy Days

This miniature quilt is small enough to fit on any wall. Paper foundation piecing helps keep the bright pinwheel blocks spinning in precise formation. For a foundation piecing lesson, see *Sew Easy: Paper Foundation Piecing* on page 37.

PROJECT RATING: INTERMEDIATE

Size: 14½" × 18¼"

Blocks: 12 (3") Pinwheel blocks

MATERIALS

1 fat eighth★ blue print #1 for blocks

⅜ yard white fabric for blocks

1 fat eighth★ medium blue print for outer border

⅜ yard blue print #2 for sashing strips, inner border, and binding

12 (2½" × 5") rectangles bright print fabrics for blocks

1 (3" × 6") rectangle multi-color print for sashing squares

18" × 22" piece of backing fabric

18" × 22" piece of batting

Windy Days Printed Foundation Sheets or tracing paper

★fat eighth = 9" × 20"

Cutting

Patterns for paper piecing are on page 85. Measurements include ¼" seam allowances. Border strips are exact length needed. You may want to make them longer to allow for piecing variations.

From blue print #1, cut:

• 3 (2½"-wide) strips. From strips, cut 24 (2½") squares. Cut squares in half diagonally to make 48 triangles for piece #1.

From white fabric, cut:

• 2 (3"-wide) strips. From strips, cut 48 (1" × 3") rectangles for piece #2.

• 2 (2½"-wide) strips. From strips, cut 24 (2½") squares. Cut squares in half diagonally to make 48 triangles for piece #3.

From medium blue print, cut:

• 4 (1¾"-wide) strips. From strips, cut 2 (1¾" × 16¼") side outer borders and 2 (1¾" × 15") top and bottom outer borders.

From blue print #2, cut:

• 2 (2¼"-wide) strips for binding.

• 4 (1¼"-wide) strips. From strips, cut 2 (1¼" × 14¾") side inner borders, 2 (1¼" × 12½") top and bottom inner borders, and 17 (1¼" × 3½") sashing strips.

From each bright rectangle, cut:

• 2 (2½") squares. Cut squares in half diagonally to make 4 triangles for piece #4. You will have a total of 12 sets of 4 triangles.

From multi-color print, cut:

• 6 (1¼") sashing squares.

Block Assembly

1. To make 1 block, trace 4 each of Unit 1 Foundation Pattern and Unit 2 Foundation Pattern onto tracing paper. Roughly cut out patterns.

2. Refer to *Sew Easy: Paper Foundation Piecing* on page 37 to paper piece Units 1 and 2.

3. Referring to *Block Assembly Diagram,* join 1 Unit 1 and 1 Unit 2 to make a quadrant. Make 4 quadrants. Join into rows; join rows to complete 1 Pinwheel block *(Block Diagram).* Make 12 blocks.

Unit 1 Diagram

Unit 2 Diagram

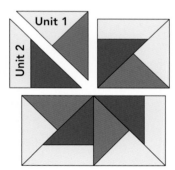

Block Assembly Diagram

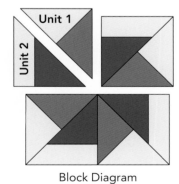

Block Diagram

Quilt Top Assembly Diagram

Quilt Assembly

1. Referring to *Quilt Top Assembly Diagram,* lay out blocks, sashing strips, and sashing squares. Join into horizontal rows; join rows to complete quilt center.

2. Add side inner borders to quilt center. Add top and bottom inner borders to quilt. Repeat for outer borders.

Finishing

1. Layer backing, batting, and quilt top; baste. Quilt as desired. Quilt shown was quilted with an allover meandering design *(Quilting Diagram on page 85).*

2. Join 2¼"-wide blue print #2 strips into 1 continuous strip for straight-grain French-fold binding. Add binding to quilt.

Quilting Diagram

DESIGNER

Patricia Kerko made her first quilt for her son Chris. He has been the inspiration for many of her projects, including this little wallhanging. ✳

Unit 1 Foundation Pattern

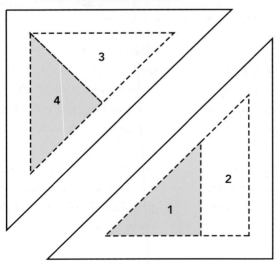

Unit 2 Foundation Pattern

Pineapple Salsa

Designer Nancy Mahoney used bold and lively batiks to make the Pineapple block in a non-traditional way.

PROJECT RATING: INTERMEDIATE
Size: 74" × 74"
Blocks: 36 (10") Pineapple blocks

MATERIALS

½ yard **each** of 12 assorted batiks in brown, green, orange, and blue

⅜ yard red batik for blocks

5¼ yards cream batik for blocks and borders

2 yards navy batik for borders and binding

Paper for foundations

4½ yards backing fabric

Full-size quilt batting

Cutting

Measurements include ¼" seam allowances. Border strips are exact length needed. You may want to make them longer to allow for piecing variations. Foundation pattern is on page 91. See *Sew Easy: Paper Foundation Piecing* on page 37 for instructions on paper foundation piecing.

NOTE: Pieces are cut over-size for foundation piecing.

From each of 3 assorted brown batiks, cut:

• 2 (3¾"-wide) strips. From strips, cut 18 (3¾") squares. Cut squares in half diagonally to make 36 half-square triangles for foundation piecing (pieces #7, #16, and #25).

From each of 3 assorted green batiks, cut:

• 3 (5½"-wide) strips. From strips, cut 18 (5½") squares. Cut squares in half diagonally to make 36 half-square triangles for foundation piecing (pieces #6, #15, and #24).

From each of 3 assorted orange batiks, cut:

• 3 (5½"-wide) strips. From strips, cut 18 (5½") squares. Cut squares in half diagonally to make 36 half-square triangles for foundation piecing (pieces #8, #17, and #22).

From each of 3 assorted blue batiks, cut:

• 3 (5½"-wide) strips. From strips, cut 18 (5½") squares. Cut squares in half diagonally to make 36 half-square triangles for foundation piecing (pieces #9, #14 and #23).

From red batik, cut:

• 3 (3"-wide) strips. From strips, cut 36 (3") squares for foundation piecing (piece #1).

From cream batik, cut:

• 4 (4¾"-wide) strips. From strips, cut 32 (4¾") squares. Cut squares in half diagonally to make 64 half-square A triangles.

• 7 (3½"-wide) strips. From strips, cut 72 (3½") squares. Cut squares in half diagonally to make 144 half-square triangles for foundation piecing (pieces #2, #3, #4, and #5).

- 29 (2¾"-wide) strips. From strips, cut 144 (2¾" × 7¾") rectangles for foundation piecing (pieces #18, #19, #20, and #21).
- 21 (2¼"-wide) strips. From strips, cut 144 (2¼" × 5½") rectangles for foundation piecing (pieces #10, #11, #12, and #13).
- 8 (1½"-wide) strips. Piece strips to make 2 (1½" × 60½") side inner borders and 2 (1½" × 62½") top and bottom inner borders.

From navy batik, cut:
- 4 (4¾"-wide) strips. From strips, cut 32 (4¾") squares. Cut squares in half diagonally to make 64 half-square A triangles.
- 1 (4⅜"-wide) strip. From strip, cut 4 (4⅜") B squares.
- 8 (2½"-wide) strips. Piece strips to make 2 (2½" × 70¼") side outer borders and 2 (2½" × 74¼") top and bottom outer borders.
- 9 (2¼"-wide) strips for binding.

Block Assembly

1. Enlarge foundation pattern 200%. Trace 36 foundation patterns.

Sew **Smart**™

The blocks are larger than a regular piece of paper. Tape your enlarged pattern pieces together. Trace onto 1 (11") square of tracing paper. Staple 5 paper squares to the traced square. Using an old 90/14 needle in sewing machine, and no thread, stitch on all the lines to create 6 paper foundations. Before using each foundation, add the numbers for the sewing sequence. You may want to note the color placement, too. Repeat to make the required number of foundations. —Nancy

2. Foundation piece block in numerical order (*Block Diagram*). Make 36 blocks.

Block Diagram

Pieced Border Assembly

1. Join 1 cream A triangle and 1 navy A triangle as shown in *Triangle-Square Diagrams*. Make 64 triangle-squares.

Triangle-Square Diagrams

2. Referring to *Quilt Top Assembly Diagram*, join 16 triangle-squares to make 1 pieced border. Make 4 pieced borders.

Quilt Assembly

1. Lay out blocks as shown in *Quilt Top Assembly Diagram*. Join into rows; join rows to complete quilt center.
2. Add cream side inner borders to quilt center. Add top and bottom inner borders to quilt.
3. Add pieced borders to sides of quilt.
4. Add 1 navy B square to each end of remaining pieced borders. Add borders to top and bottom of quilt.
5. Add navy side outer borders to quilt center. Add top and bottom outer borders to quilt.

Finishing

1. Divide backing into 2 (2¼-yard) lengths. Cut 1 piece in half lengthwise to make 2 narrow panels. Join 1 narrow panel to each side of wider panel; press seam allowances toward narrow panels.
2. Layer backing, batting, and quilt top; baste. Quilt as desired. Quilt shown was quilted with an allover design (*Quilting Diagram*).
3. Join 2¼"-wide navy strips into 1 continuous piece for straight-grain French-fold binding. Add binding to quilt.

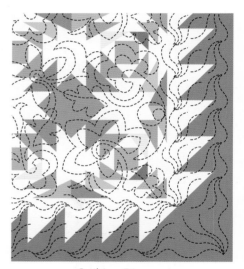

Quilting Diagram

Quilt Top Assembly Diagram

TRIED & TRUE

Our version of this block features prints in autumn hues.

Fabrics shown are from the A Simpler Time collection

by Holly Taylor for Moda.

DESIGNER

Designer Nancy Mahoney is a quilting teacher, fabric designer, and author of ten books. She enjoys making traditional quilts using new techniques that make quiltmaking easy and fun. ✳

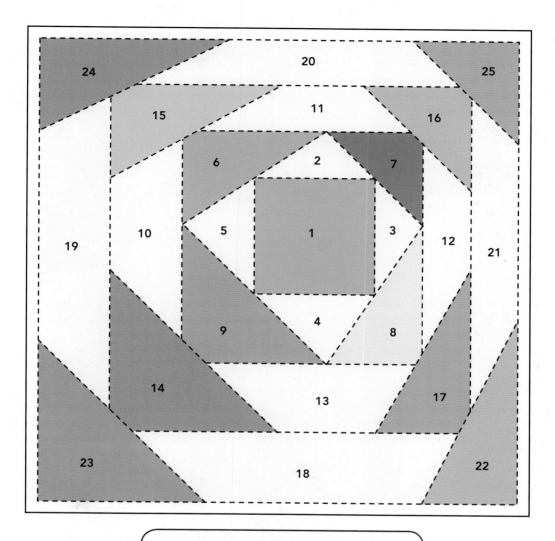

ENLARGE FOUNDATION 200%
Permission is granted by
Love of Quilting to enlarge and make
copies of this pattern.

Pineapple Punch Pincushion

PROJECT RATING: INTERMEDIATE

Size: 3½" square

MATERIALS

Assorted dark print scraps
Assorted light print scraps
4" square backing fabric
2 (4") squares muslin for lining
Paper for foundation
Sand or other filler

Cutting

Measurements include ¼" seam allowances. Pieces for foundation piecing are cut oversize.

From assorted dark prints, cut a total of:

• 4 (1¼" × 4½") D rectangles.
• 4 (1¼" × 3½") C rectangles.
• 4 (1¼" × 2½") B rectangles.
• 4 (1¼") A squares.

From assorted light prints, cut a total of:

• 17 (1½") A squares.

Block Assembly

1. Trace or photocopy Pineapple Foundation.

2. Referring to photo, paper piece foundation in numerical order using assorted light and dark prints.

Pincushion Assembly

1. Layer 1 muslin square, backing square (right side up), pieced block (right side down), and 1 muslin square.

Stitch around edge, using a ¼" seam allowance and leaving a 2" opening in one side. Backstitch at beginning and end of seam.

2. Turn pincushion right side out. Fill with sand; hand stitch opening closed.

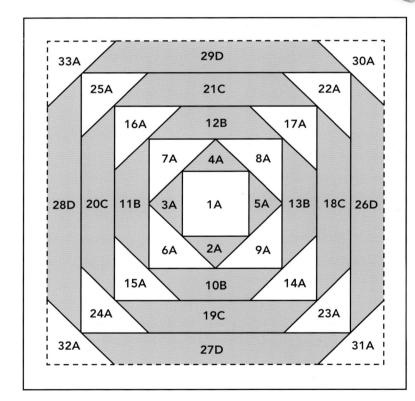

Pineapple Foundation

DESIGNER

Julie Letvin started her quilt company, Me & My Stitches, in 2008. In addition to her foundation-pieced pincushions, she makes tiny quilt blocks and encases them in glass, creating miniature quilt jewelry. ✳

Flag Fanatic Pincushion

Size: 3½" × 2¾"

MATERIALS

5" square red print for stripes
5" square cream print for stripes
1 (1½" × 2½") rectangle navy print
  for star field
5" square cream-and-navy print
4" × 3" rectangle backing fabric
2 (4" × 3") rectangles muslin
  for lining
Paper for foundation
Sand

Cutting

Measurements include ¼" seam allowances. Pieces for foundation piecing are cut oversize.

From red print square, cut:
• 4 (1"-wide) strips.

From cream print, cut:
• 4 (1"-wide) strips.

From cream-and-navy print, cut:
• 2 (1¼"-wide) strips.

Block Assembly

1. Trace or photocopy Flag Foundation.
2. Referring to photo, paper piece foundation in numerical order using red, cream, navy, and cream-and-navy prints.

Pincushion Assembly

1. Layer 1 muslin rectangle, backing rectangle (right side up), pieced block (right side down), and 1 muslin rectangle. Stitch around edge, using a ¼" seam allowance and leaving a 2" opening in one side. Backstitch at beginning and end of seam.
2. Turn pincushion right side out. Fill with sand; hand stitch opening closed.

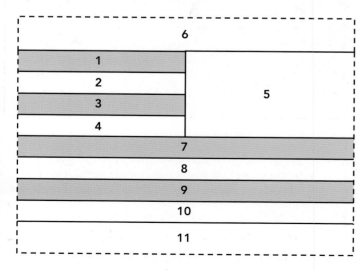

Flag Foundation

FLAG
FARM 2003

Diane
Hansen

It's a Small Honor

Make this scrappy patriotic miniature quilt using paper foundation piecing.
For a distinctive display, mount your little quilt in a picture frame
as designer Diane Hansen did.

PROJECT RATING: INTERMEDIATE
Finished Size: 4" × 6"

MATERIALS

Scraps of red, navy, green, brown,
gold, and light prints
1 fat quarter★ gold print for border,
binding, and backing
5" × 7" piece of flannel for batting
Paper for foundations
★fat quarter = 18" × 20"

Cutting

Measurements include ¼" seam allowances.
Border strips are exact length needed.
You may want to make them longer to
allow for piecing variations. Foundation
patterns are on pages 96–97.

From gold print, cut:
• 2 (1"-wide) strips. From strips, cut
  2 (1" × 6½") side borders and
  2 (1" × 3½") top and bottom borders.
• 2 (1¾"-wide) strips for binding.
• 1 (5" × 7") rectangle for backing.

From scraps, cut:
• Pieces as needed for foundation piecing.
  Cut pieces at least ½" larger than the
  section to be covered.

Foundation Piecing

1. Trace or photocopy foundation patterns for Flag Unit, Units A and B,
   and Star Units 1, 2, and 3 on pages
   96 and 97.
2. Referring to *Sew Easy: Paper Foundation Piecing* on page 37 and *Quilt
   Top Assembly Diagrams,* foundation
   piece units in numerical order.

Star Assembly

1. Lay out Star Units as shown in *Star
   Assembly Diagrams.*
2. Join Star Units to complete Star.

Star Unit 1

Star Unit 2

Star Unit 3

Star Assembly Diagrams

Quilt Assembly

1. Lay out Star, Flag Unit, and A and B Units as shown in *Quilt Top Assembly Diagrams*. Join into sections. Join sections to complete quilt center.

2. Add gold borders to top and bottom of quilt. Add gold borders to sides of quilt.

Finishing

1. Layer backing, flannel, and quilt top; baste. Quilt shown was not quilted because of its small size.

2. Join 1¾"-wide gold print strips into 1 continuous piece for straight-grain French-fold binding. Add binding to quilt.

3. Quilt shown was mounted on a fabric-covered board and set in an 8" × 10" frame.

Unit A

Flag Unit

Unit A

Unit B

Unit A

Quilt Top Assembly Diagrams

DESIGNER

Diane Hansen is a fourth-generation quilter who enjoys making patriotic scrap quilts. She has combined these two loves by designing a line of patterns for patriotic wallhangings. ✳

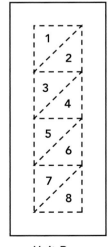

Unit B

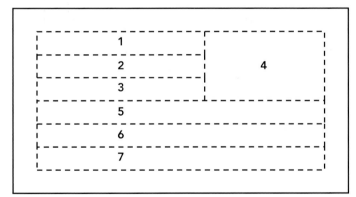

Flag Unit

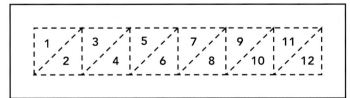

Unit A

Star Unit 1

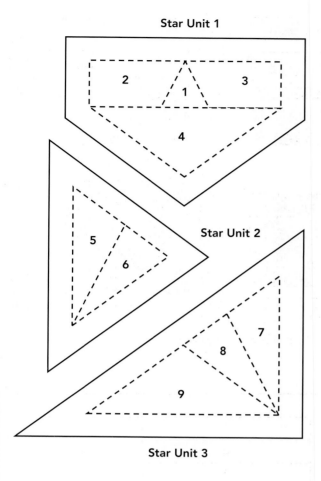

Star Unit 2

Star Unit 3

Kinkame

Foundation piecing enables you to accurately piece the small units in this quilt.

PROJECT RATING: CHALLENGING
Size: 35½" × 36½"
Blocks: 45 Hexagon blocks

MATERIALS

11 fat eighths★ assorted light prints in tan, green, lavender, and blue for blocks

11 fat eighths★ assorted dark prints in taupe, brown, and green for blocks

1¼ yards cream print for block backgrounds

⅞ yard dark taupe print for large triangles and outer border

⅝ yard tan print for inner border

½ yard light plaid for outer border

½ yard dark plaid for binding

Paper for foundation piecing

Template material

1¼ yards backing fabric

Crib-size quilt batting

★fat eighth = 9" × 20"

Cutting

Measurements include ¼" seam allowances. Border strips are exact length needed. You may want to make them longer to allow for piecing variations. Pieces A, B, and C are cut over-sized for foundation piecing. Patterns for D triangle and foundations are on page 101.

NOTE: For instructions on paper foundation piecing, see *Sew Easy*: Paper Foundation Piecing on page 37.

From light print fat eighths, cut a total of:
• 18 (2¼"-wide) strips. From strips, cut 135 (2¼") A squares.
• 22 (1½"-wide) strips. From strips, cut 258 (1½") B squares.

From dark print fat eighths, cut a total of:
• 18 (2¼"-wide) strips. From strips, cut 135 (2¼") A squares.
• 22 (1½"-wide) strips. From strips, cut 258 (1½") B squares.

From cream print, cut:
• 11 (2"-wide) strips. From strips, cut 258 (2" x 1½") C rectangles.
• 11 (1½"-wide) strips. From strips, cut 258 (1½") B squares.

From dark taupe print, cut:
• 5 (2¾"-wide) strips. From strips, cut 92 D triangles.
• 8 (1½"-wide) strips. From strips, cut 192 (1½") B squares.
• 2 (1⅝") squares. Cut squares in half diagonally to make 4 half-square E triangles.

From tan print, cut:
• 4 (4⅛"-wide) strips for inner borders.

From light plaid, cut:
• 8 (1½"-wide) strips. From strips, cut 192 (1½") B squares.
• 2 (1⅝") squares. Cut squares in half diagonally to make 4 half-square E triangles.

From dark plaid, cut:
• 2¼"-wide bias strips. Join to make about 170" of bias for binding.

Block Assembly

1. Trace or photocopy 90 Section 1, 123 Section 2, 123 Section 3, and 32 Section 4 from patterns on page 101.

2. Choose 3 matching dark A squares, 3 matching light A squares, 6 matching dark B squares, 6 matching light B squares, 6 cream B squares, and 6 cream C rectangles.

3. Foundation piece 2 Section 1, 3 Section 2, and 3 Section 3 as shown in *Block Assembly Diagrams*. Lay out sections; join to complete 1 block *(Block Diagram)*. Make 39 blocks.

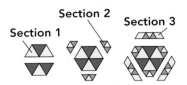

Block Assembly Diagrams

Block Diagram

4. Choose 3 matching dark A squares, 3 matching light A squares, 4 matching dark B squares, 4 matching light B squares, 4 cream B squares, and 4 cream C rectangles.

5. Foundation piece 2 Section 1, 2 Section 2, and 2 Section 3. Lay out sections as shown in *Side Block Assembly Diagrams*. Join to complete 1 Side block *(Side Block Diagram)*. Make 6 Side blocks.

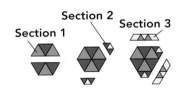

Side Block Assembly Diagrams

Side Block Diagram

Outer Border Assembly

1. Foundation piece 32 Section 4 using light plaid print B squares and dark taupe print B squares.

2. Join 8 Section 4 as shown in *Quilt Top Assembly Diagram* to complete 1 outer border. Make 4 outer borders.

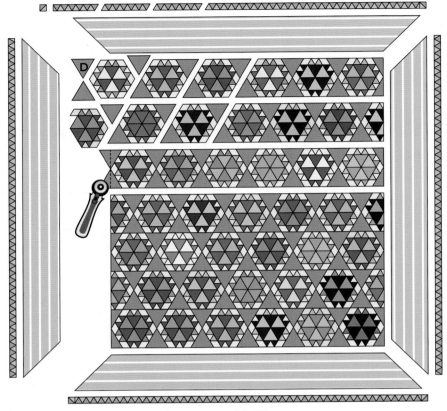

Section 4   Section 4

Quilt Top Assembly Diagram

Quilt Assembly

1. Lay out blocks, Side blocks, and dark taupe print D triangles as shown in *Quilt Top Assembly Diagram*. Join into rows; join rows to complete quilt center.

2. Trim side blocks and D triangles as shown in *Quilt Top Assembly Diagram*, leaving a ¼" seam allowance beyond points of blocks.

3. Add tan print inner borders to quilt, mitering corners.

4. Measure length of quilt. Trim 2 outer borders to that measurement.

5. Measure width of quilt. Trim remaining outer borders to that measurement.

6. Join 1 dark taupe E triangle and 1 light plaid E triangle as shown in *Triangle-Square Diagrams*. Make 4 triangle-squares.

Triangle-Square Diagrams

7. Add side outer borders to quilt.

8. Add 1 triangle-square to each end of top and bottom outer borders. Add borders to quilt.

Finishing

1. Layer backing, batting, and quilt top; baste. Quilt as desired. Quilt shown was quilted with hexagons in blocks and parallel lines in triangles and inner border *(Quilting Diagram on page 101)*.

2. Add binding to quilt.

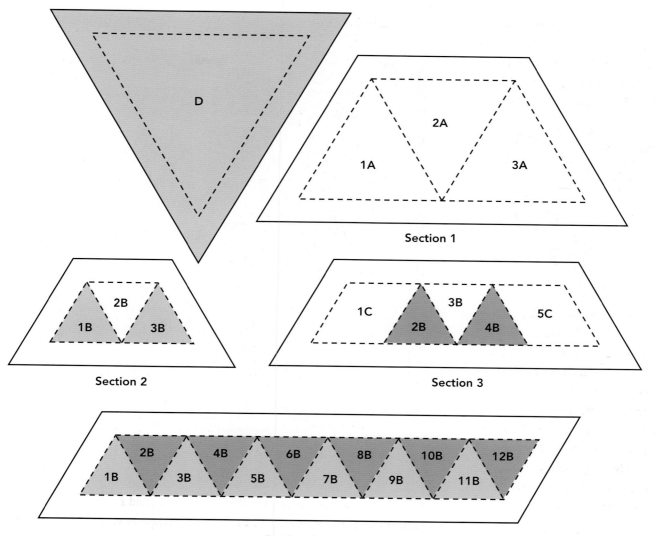

D

2A

1A   3A

Section 1

2B

1B   3B

Section 2

1C   3B   5C

2B   4B

Section 3

2B   4B   6B   8B   10B   12B

1B   3B   5B   7B   9B   11B

Section 4

Quilting Diagram

TRIED & TRUE

This design has a cottage chic look in fabrics from the Supporting Cast collection by Ro Gregg for Northcott.

DESIGNER

Kumiko Maeda loves antique quilts, and hopes that more people learn about quilts and become quilters. About Kinkame, she says she wanted to make a quilt with "beauty of the simple moment." ✻

Schoolhouse

This traditional quilt, in the popular Schoolhouse pattern, is from the collection of the International Quilt Study Center & Museum in Lincoln, Nebraska. Fabrics in the quilt have been reproduced by Andover Fabrics so you can make a new version of this antique quilt.

PROJECT RATING: INTERMEDIATE

Size: 70" × 79"

Blocks: 28 (9") Schoolhouse blocks

MATERIALS

5 fat quarters★ assorted black prints

4 fat quarters★ assorted blue prints

7 fat quarters★ assorted light stripes for doors, windows, and house trim

1 fat quarter★ red print for chimneys

2¾ yards cream solid

2¾ yards black stripe for setting squares and outer border

Paper for foundation piecing

5 yards backing fabric

Twin-size quilt batting

★fat quarter = 18" × 20"

Cutting

Measurements include ¼" seam allowances. Border strips are exact length needed. You may want to make them longer to allow for piecing variations. Pattern for Roof foundation is on page 105. For instructions on paper piecing, see *Sew Easy: Foundation Paper Piecing* on page 37. Pieces for foundation piecing are cut over sized.

From each black print fat quarter, cut:

• 1 (2½"-wide) strip. From strip, cut 4 (2½" × 4") D rectangles for foundation piecing.

• 2 (2"-wide) strips. From strips, cut 4 (2" × 7") A rectangles for foundation piecing.

• 3 (1½"-wide) strips. From strips, cut 8 (1½" × 4½") H rectangles and 4 (1½" × 3¼") K rectangles.

• 2 (1⅜"-wide) strips. From strips, cut 8 (1⅜" × 4") J rectangles.

• 2 (1¼"-wide) strips. From strips, cut 12 (1¼" × 3") F rectangles.

From each blue print fat quarter, cut:

• 1 (2½"-wide) strip. From strip, cut 2 (2½" × 4") D rectangles for foundation piecing.

• 1 (2"-wide) strip. From strip, cut 2 (2" × 7") A rectangles for foundation piecing.

• 2 (1½"-wide) strips. From strips, cut 4 (1½" × 4½") H rectangles and 2 (1½" × 3¼") K rectangles.

• 1 (1⅜"-wide) strip. From strip, cut 4 (1⅜" × 4") J rectangles.

• 1 (1¼"-wide) strip. From strip, cut 6 (1¼" × 3") F rectangles.

From each light stripe fat quarter, cut:

• 1 (1½"-wide) strip. From strip, cut 4 (1½" × 4") I rectangles.

• 2 (1⅜"-wide) strips. From strips, cut 8 (1⅜" × 3") G rectangles.

• 4 (¾"-wide) strips. From strips, cut 8 (¾" × 5") B rectangles for house front and foundation piecing and 4 (¾" × 3½") C rectangles for foundation piecing.

From red print fat quarter, cut:

• 5 (1⅜"-wide) strips. From strips, cut 56 (1⅜" × 1½") O rectangles.

From cream solid, cut:

• 2 (2¾"-wide) strips. From strips, cut 28 (2¾") squares. Cut squares in half diagonally to make 56 half-square E triangles for foundation piecing.

• 16 (2¼"-wide) strips. Piece strips to make 2 (2¼" × 72½") side inner borders and 2 (2¼" × 67") top and bottom inner borders. Remaining strips are for binding.

• 32 (1½"-wide) strips. From strips, cut 56 (1½" × 9½") R rectangles,

56 (1½" × 7½") Q rectangles, 28 (1½" × 3¼") L rectangles, 28 (1½" × 2") M rectangles, and 28 (1½") N squares.

From black stripe, cut:

• 4 (2¼"-wide) **lengthwise** strips. From strips, cut 2 (2¼" × 76") side outer borders and 2 (2¼" × 70½") top and bottom outer borders.

From remainder of black stripe, cut:

• 10 (9½"-wide) **crosswise** strips. From strips, cut 28 (9½") S squares.

Block Assembly

1. Trace or photocopy 28 Roof Unit foundations from pattern on page 105.

2. Referring to *Roof Unit Diagram*, paper piece foundations in numerical order. Make 28 Roof Units.

   NOTE: You will make 1 Roof Unit, 1 Side Unit, and 1 Front Unit for each block. Use matching black or blue print pieces for house, matching light stripe pieces for door and windows, and matching light stripe pieces for narrow trim (B and C pieces) to make the units for each block.

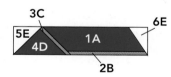

Roof Unit Diagram

3. Lay out 3 matching black or blue print F rectangles and 2 H rectangles, and 2 light stripe G rectangles as shown in *Side Unit Assembly Diagrams*. Join to complete 1 Side Unit. Make 28 Side Units.

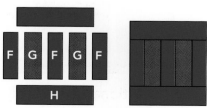

Side Unit Assembly Diagrams

4. Lay out 2 matching black or blue print J rectangles and 1 K rectangle, 1 light stripe I rectangle, and 1 light stripe B rectangle as shown in *Front Unit Assembly Diagrams*. Join to complete 1 Front Unit. Make 28 Front Units.

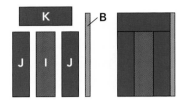

Front Unit Assembly Diagrams

5. Join 1 cream solid L rectangle, 1 cream solid M rectangle, 1 cream solid N square, and 2 red print O rectangles as shown in *Chimney Unit Diagrams*. Make 28 Chimney Units.

Chimney Unit Assembly Diagrams

6. Lay out 1 Roof Unit, 1 Chimney Unit, 1 Front Unit, 1 Side Unit, 2 cream solid Q rectangles, and 2 cream solid R rectangles as shown in *House Block Assembly Diagram*. Join to complete 1 House block *(House Block Diagram)*. Make 28 House blocks.

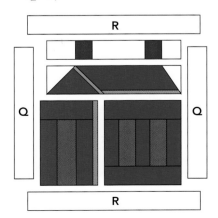

House Block Assembly Diagram

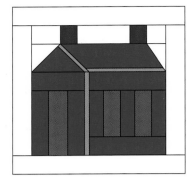

House Block Diagram

Quilt Assembly

1. Lay out blocks and black stripe S squares as shown in *Quilt Top Assembly Diagram*. Join into rows; join rows to complete quilt center.

2. Add cream solid side inner borders to quilt center. Add top and bottom inner borders to quilt.

3. Repeat for black print outer borders.

Finishing

1. Divide backing into 2 (2½-yard) lengths. Cut 1 piece in half lengthwise to make 2 narrow panels. Join 1 narrow panel to each side of wider panel; press seam allowances toward narrow panels.

2. Layer backing, batting, and quilt top; baste. Quilt as desired. Quilt shown was quilted with diagonal parallel lines *(Quilting Diagram on page 105)*.

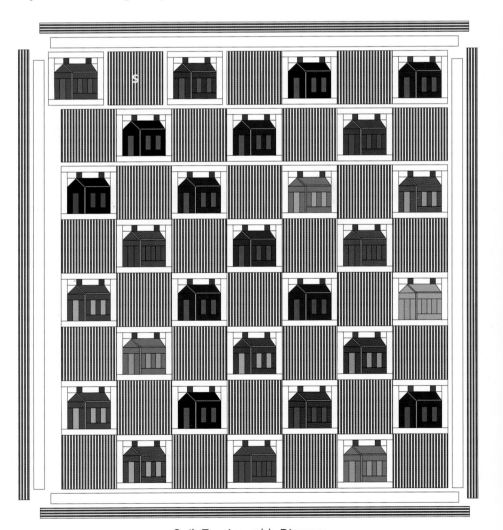

Quilt Top Assembly Diagram

3. Join 2¼"-wide cream solid strips into 1 continuous piece for straight-grain French-fold binding. Add binding to quilt.

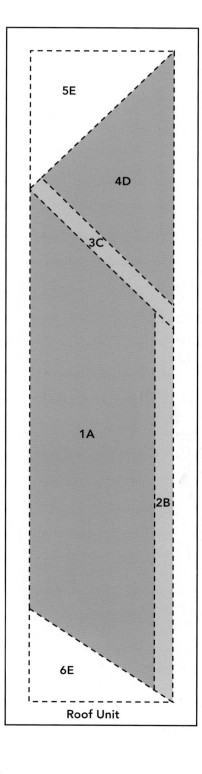

Roof Unit

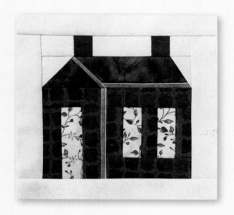

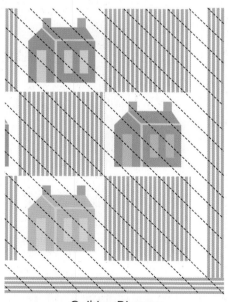

Quilting Diagram

QUILT MADE BY **Marianne Fons, Bettina Havig, Marti Michell, Liz Porter, and Judy Martin.**

MACHINE QUILTED BY **Jean Nolte.**

Happy Home

Marianne Fons intentionally surprised the other participants at the beginning of this round-robin project. "I figured they would expect a traditional center from me, so I created a funky house block with pinwheel corners. My friends Bettina Havig, Marti Michell, Liz Porter, and Judy Martin added the creative borders and appliqués."

PROJECT RATING: CHALLENGING

Size: 51" × 51"

MATERIALS

Scraps of yellow, orange, red, purple, blue, green, pink, black, and black-and-white prints for houses, trees, pinwheels, stars, and appliqués

¼ yard each of 1 turquoise, 5 blue, and 4 green prints for borders

¼ yard rainbow stripe for Pinwheel Border

¼ yard small black-and-white check for House and Tree Border

½ yard sky print for House and Tree Border

⅓ yard white for Checkerboard Border

⅓ yard black for Checkerboard Border

1½ yards black print for prairie points

Optional: Paper-backed fusible web

3⅓ yards backing fabric

Twin-size batting

CENTER HOUSE
Cutting

Measurements include ¼" seam allowances.

From yellow print, cut:

- 6 (1½") A squares for windows.

From orange print, cut:

- 6 (1½") A squares for windows.

From black-and-white print #1, cut:

- 2 (4½" × 1¾") B rectangles for house front.
- 1 (4½" × 2½") C rectangle for house front.
- 1 (5½") square for paper piecing roof section H.

From black-and-white print #2, cut:

- 1 (11½" × 5") rectangle for roof section G.

From black-and-white print #3, cut:

- 2 (3½" × 5½") rectangles for roof section I.
- 2 (2½") J squares.
- 1 (5½" × 2½") K rectangle.

From red print, cut:

- 1 (4½" × 2") D rectangle for door.

From black-with-multi-colors print, cut:

- 2 (8½" × 2½") E rectangles for house side.
- 2 (1½" × 2½") F rectangles for house side.

From black-with-red print, cut:

- 2 (2" × 2½") L rectangles for chimneys.

From green print, cut:

- 1 (2½" × 12½") M rectangle for grass.

Roof Assembly

1. Draw a 4" × 12" rectangle on tracing paper or other lightweight paper.
2. Referring to *Center House Roof Foundation* on page 113, draw lines as shown. (Pattern is reversed for paper foundation piecing.)
3. Use paper foundation piecing to assemble roof section. Piece in alphabetical order.
4. Trim roof section to 4½" × 12½", trimming on outer drawn lines of paper pattern. Remove paper.

House Assembly

1. Join 2 yellow A squares and 2 orange A squares to form a four patch window unit. Make 3 window units.

2. Referring to *Center House Assembly Diagram*, join 1 B rectangle to each long side of D rectangle for door unit. Add C rectangle to top edge. Join 3 window units to 2 F rectangles, alternating pieces. Add 1 E rectangle to top edge and 1 E rectangle to bottom edge of window section. Join window unit to door unit.

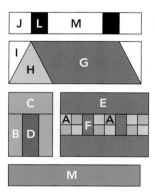

Center House Assembly Diagram

3. Join 2 J, 1 K, and 2 L, to make chimney unit.

4. Join green rectangle M, door/window unit, roof unit, and chimney unit to complete Center House.

PINWHEEL BORDER
Cutting

From yellow print and black-and-white print, cut:

• 8 (2⅜") squares for pinwheels. Cut each square in half diagonally to make 16 yellow and 16 black-and-white half-square A triangles.

From rainbow stripe, cut:

• 2 (3½"-wide) strips. From strips, cut 2 (3½" × 14½") rectangles for side borders and 2 (3½" × 12½") rectangles for top and bottom borders.

Border Assembly

1. Join 1 yellow A triangle and 1 black-and-white A triangle to make a triangle-square. Make 16 triangle-squares.

2. Referring to *Pinwheel Diagrams*, join 4 triangle-squares to make Pinwheel block. Make 4 Pinwheel blocks.

Pinwheel Diagrams

3. Referring to *Pinwheel Border Assembly Diagram*, add striped borders to sides of Center House. Join 1 Pinwheel block to each end of top and bottom striped borders. Join to top and bottom of quilt.

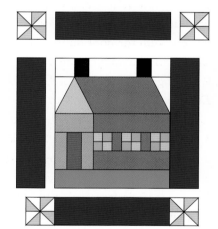

Pinwheel Border Assembly Diagram

SKY AND GRASS BORDER
Cutting

Patterns for appliqué pieces are on page 115.

From green print, cut:

• 1 (4" × 24½") A rectangle for bottom border.

• 2 (3½") B squares for side border.

From turquoise print, cut:

• 1 (3½"-wide) strip. From strip, cut 2 (3½" × 17½") C rectangles for side borders.

• 1 (4½" × 24½") D rectangle for top border.

From assorted prints, cut:

• Appliqué pieces for 1 chicken, 1 cat, 1 sun, 2 trees, and 3 clouds.

Border Assembly

1. Referring to *Sky and Grass Border Assembly Diagrams,* join B squares to C rectangles. Join these borders to sides of center. Add A rectangle to bottom and D rectangle to top of center.

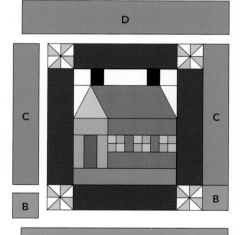

Sky and Grass Border Assembly Diagrams

2. Referring to *Sky and Grass Border Assembly Diagrams,* appliqué chicken, cat, sun, trees, and clouds on border.

SMALL COTTAGE
Cutting

From assorted prints, cut 5 sets of:

- 2 (1" × 3") A rectangles and 1 (1½" × 1⅛") B rectangle for cottage front.
- 1 (1½" × 2⅜") C rectangle for door.
- 2 (1½" × 3") D rectangles and 2 (1½" × 1⅛") F rectangles for cottage side.
- 1 (1½" × 1¾") E rectangle for window.
- 1 (6" × 3") rectangle for paper piecing roof section G.
- 1 (3") square for paper piecing roof section H.
- 2 (2" × 3") rectangles sky fabric for paper piecing roof section I.

From sky prints, cut:

- 6 (2⅝" × 1¼") J rectangles.
- 2 (3¾" × 1¼") L rectangles.
- 2 (1½" × 1¼") M rectangles.

From red print, cut:

- 5 (1¼") K squares for chimneys.

Roof Assembly

1. Draw a 1¾" × 5" rectangle on tracing paper or other lightweight paper.

2. Referring to *Small Cottage Roof Foundation* on page 114, make 2 paper foundations as shown and 2 reversed.

3. Use paper foundation piecing to form roof section. Piece in alphabetical order.

4. Trim roof section to 2¼" × 5½", trimming on outer drawn lines of paper pattern.

Chimney Unit 1

Chimney Unit 2

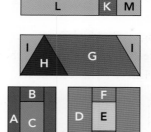  

MAKE 2 AS SHOWN AND 1 REVERSED

MAKE 1 AS SHOWN AND 1 REVERSED

Small Cottage Assembly Diagrams

Cottage Assembly

1. Choose 1 cut set and, referring to *Small Cottage Assembly Diagrams,* join B to top of C. Add 1 A to each long side to complete door unit.

2. Add 1 F to top and bottom of E. Join 1 D rectangle to each side to complete window unit. Join window unit to door unit. Make 2 door/window sections with the door on the right, and 3 with the door on the left.

3. Referring to *Small Cottage Assembly Diagrams,* join 2 J and 1 K to make Chimney Unit 1. Join 1 K, 1 L, and 1 M to make Chimney Unit 2. Make 3 Chimney Unit 1, 1 Chimney Unit 2, and 1 Chimney Unit 2 reversed.

4. Join a door/window section to each roof unit. (Refer to *Cottage and Tree Border Assembly Diagram* on page 110 for roof/chimney combinations.) Attach roof/chimney sections to door/window sections for 3 cottages as shown.

ROW HOUSES
Cutting

From assorted prints, cut 3 sets of:

- 2 (1" × 2⅞") A rectangles and 1 (1½" × 1¼") B rectangle for front.

- 1 (1½" × 2⅛") C rectangle for door.
- 1 (3") square for paper piecing roof section D, F, or H.

From turquoise print, cut:

- 2 (3") squares for paper piecing roof sections E and G.
- 2 (2" × 3") rectangles for paper piecing roof section I.

Roof Assembly

1. Referring to *Row Houses Foundation* on page 114, trace lines as shown.

2. Use paper foundation piecing to form roof section. Piece in alphabetical order.

3. Trim roof section to 2⅛" × 6½", trimming on outer drawn lines of paper pattern.

Row Houses Assembly

1. Working with 1 cut set, and referring to *Row Houses Assembly Diagram* on page 110, join B to C. Add 1 A to each long side to complete door unit. Make 3 door units and join together.

2. Join door section to roof section.

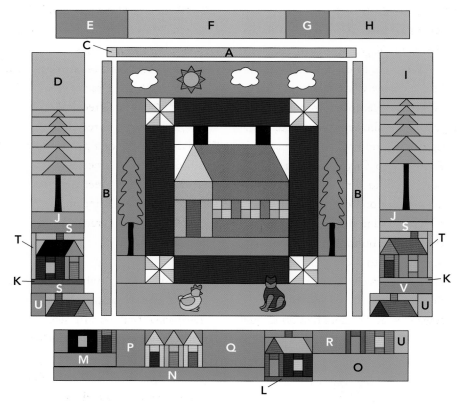

Cottage and Tree Border Assembly Diagram

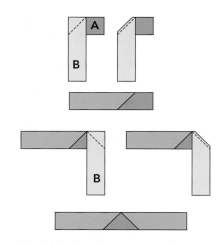

Pieced Tree Diagonal Seams Diagrams

3. Join rows to complete pieced tree top. Make 2 tree tops.

4. Referring to *Pieced Tree Assembly Diagrams*, appliqué tree trunks to M and N rectangles. Join to pieced tree tops.

COTTAGE & TREE BORDER
Cutting

From black and white check print, cut:

- 1 (1½" × 24½") A rectangle for top inner border.
- 2 (1½" × 28") B rectangles for side inner borders.

From yellow print, cut:

- 2 (1½") C squares for inner border corners.

From assorted sky prints, cut:

- 1 (6" × 6¾") D rectangle.
- 1 (3½" × 8") E rectangle.
- 1 (3½" × 17") F rectangle.
- 1 (3½" × 5") G rectangle.
- 1 (3½" × 9") H rectangle.
- 1 (6" × 5¼") I rectangle.

From assorted green prints, cut:

- 2 (1¾" × 6") J rectangles.
- 2 (1" × 6") K rectangles.
- 1 (1" × 5½") L rectangle.
- 1 (2" × 7") M rectangle.

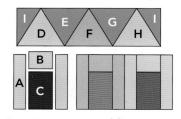

Row Houses Assembly Diagram

PIECED TREES
Cutting

From green print, cut:

- 2 (1¼" × 2") A rectangles.
- 2 (1½" × 2½") C rectangles.
- 2 (1½" × 3") E rectangles.
- 2 (1¾" × 3½") G rectangles.
- 2 (2" × 3½") I rectangles.
- 2 (2" × 4") K rectangles.

From sky print, cut:

- 4 (1¼" × 3¼") B rectangles.
- 4 (1½" × 3¼") D rectangles.
- 4 (1½" × 3") F rectangles.

- 4 (1¾" × 3") H rectangles.
- 4 (2" × 3¼") J rectangles.
- 4 (2" × 3") L rectangles.
- 1 (6" × 5½") M rectangle.
- 1 (6" × 4½") N rectangle.

From black print, cut:

- 2 tree trunks (pattern on page 115).

Tree Assembly

1. Referring to *Pieced Tree Diagonal Seams Diagrams*, place 1 B rectangle perpendicular to A rectangle. Stitch along diagonal and trim excess. Unfold and press. Repeat on other end of A with another B rectangle to complete Row 1.

2. In the same manner, combine 2 D and 1 C rectangle for Row 2, 2 F and 1 E for Row 3, 2 H and 1 G for Row 4, 2 J and 1 I for Row 5, and 2 L and 1 K for Row 6.

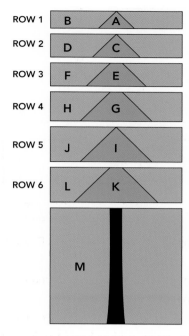

ROW 1	B A
ROW 2	D C
ROW 3	F E
ROW 4	H G
ROW 5	J I
ROW 6	L K

M

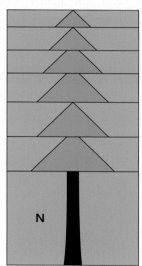

N

Pieced Tree Assembly Diagrams

- 1 (2" × 22½") N rectangle.
- 1 (3½" × 10½") O rectangle.

From assorted turquoise prints, cut:
- 1 (3½" × 4½") P rectangle.
- 1 (7" × 4½") Q rectangle.
- 1 (4" × 3") R rectangle.
- 3 (1½" × 6") S rectangles.
- 2 (1" × 5½") T rectangles.
- 4 (2" × 3") U rectangles.
- 1 (2" × 6") V rectangle.

Border Assembly

1. Referring to *Cottage and Tree Border Assembly Diagram* on page 110, join 1 B rectangle to each side of center. Join 1 yellow C square to each end of A rectangle. Join to top of center.
2. Join pieces shown to complete left, right, top, and bottom borders.
3. Referring to *Diagram 1*, join left side border to B rectangle, stitching from top of border just to dot at tip of roof. Fold under B rectangle fabric from dot to bottom corner and appliqué next to roof. Trim excess sky fabric from back. Repeat to add right side border.
4. Attach top and bottom borders to quilt.

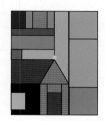

Diagram 1

CHECKERBOARD & OUTER BORDER
Cutting

From black fabric, cut:
- 6 (1½"-wide) strips.

From white fabric, cut:
- 6 (1½"-wide) strips.

From dark blue fabric for star backgrounds, cut:
- 2 (2½"-wide) strips. From strips, cut 16 (2½") A squares, 2 (2½" × 6½") C rectangles, and 1 (2½" × 4½") D rectangle.
- 1 (3½" × 6½") E rectangle.

From 1 each of yellow, orange, and red-orange fabric for stars, cut:
- 1 (2½") A square.
- 4 (2" × 3") rectangles for paper piecing B star points.

- 2 (2") squares. Cut squares in half diagonally to make 4 C triangles for paper piecing star points.

From assorted dark blue prints, cut:
- 3 (6½" × 16½") F rectangles.
- 1 (4½" × 15½") G rectangle.
- 1 (4½" × 13½") H rectangle.

From assorted green prints, cut:
- 1 (4½" × 19½") I rectangle.
- 1 (4½" × 28½") J rectangle.
- 1 (4½" × 17½") K rectangle.
- 1 (6½" × 23½") L rectangle.

Border Assembly

1. Join 1 black and 1 white 1½"-wide strip to make 1 strip set *(Checkerboard Diagrams)*. Make 6 strip sets.
2. From strip sets, cut 156 (1½"-wide) segments.
3. Join 2 segments as shown in *Checkerboard Diagrams* to make a four-patch unit.

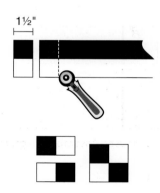

Checkerboard Diagrams

4. Join remaining segments as shown in *Checkerboard and Outer Border Assembly Diagram* on page 112. Make 2 pieced borders with 41 segments for sides, 1 border with 37 segments for bottom, and 1 border with 35 segments for top.
5. Trace Star Points Foundation on page 114. Make 8 paper foundations as shown and 4 reversed.

6. Use paper foundation piecing to form star point units. Piece in alphabetical order. For yellow star, make 1 unit as shown and 2 reversed with blue A squares, and 1 reversed using the checkerboard four-patch for the A square. For orange star, make 4 star point units as shown. For red-orange star, make 3 units as shown and 1 reversed.

7. Trim each star point unit to 2½" square, trimming on outer drawn lines of paper pattern.

8. Referring to *Checkerboard and Outer Border Assembly Diagram,* add checkerboard star point unit to left end of top checkerboard border. Add border to quilt. Add bottom and then side checkerboard borders to quilt.

9. Referring to *Checkerboard and Outer Border Assembly Diagram,* join pieces shown to complete side, top, and bottom borders. Add borders to quilt in following order: top, right, bottom, and left.

Checkerboard and Outer Border Assembly Diagram

Quilting and Finishing

1. Divide backing into 2 (1⅔-yard) lengths. Cut 1 piece in half lengthwise. Sew 1 narrow panel to 1 side of wide panel. Press seam allowances toward narrow panel. Seam will run vertically. Remaining panel is extra and may be used to make a hanging sleeve.

2. Cut 6 (8"-wide) strips from black print fabric for prairie points. Referring to *Sew Easy: Continuous Prairie Points* on page 116, add prairie points to quilt.

3. Layer backing, batting, and quilt top; baste. Quilt as desired.

4. Trim backing and batting, turn prairie points out, and turn under ¼" on quilt back. Blindstitch folded edge of quilt back to prairie points. ✳

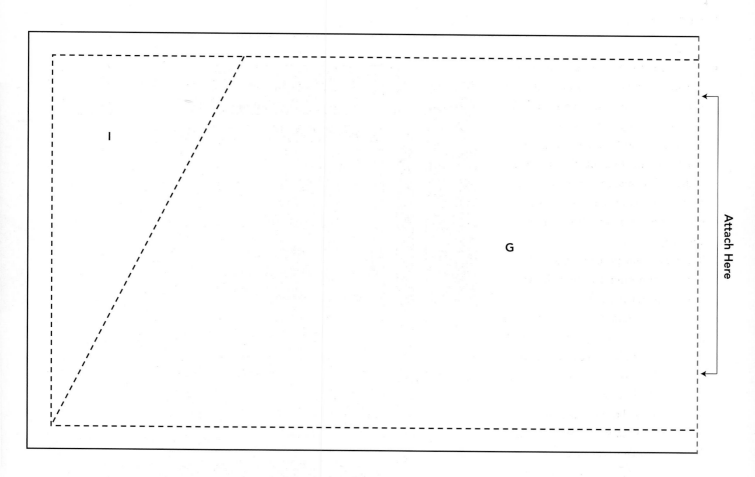

I

G

Attach Here

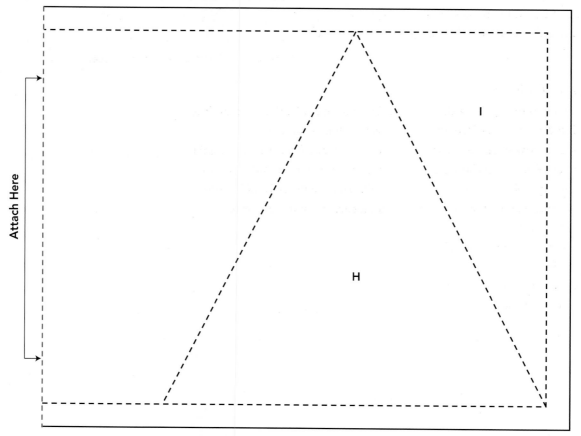

Attach Here

I

H

Center House Roof Foundation

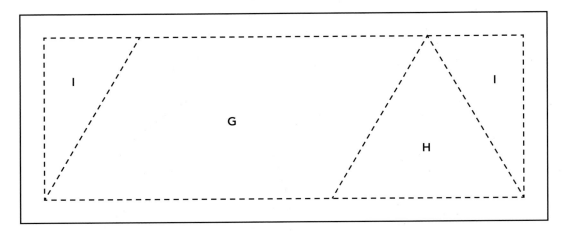

Small Cottage Roof Foundation

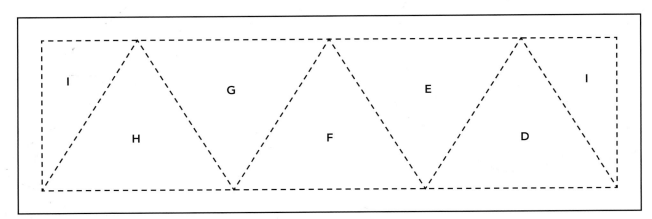

Row Houses Foundation

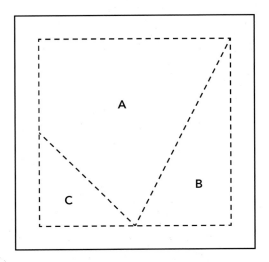

Star Points Foundation

Sun

Clouds

Tree

Chicken

Cat

Continuous Prairie Points

Try this method for continuous prairie points if you are making them all from the same fabric.

> Our instructions are for making prairie points from 4" "squares." These will fit perfectly if the dimensions of your quilt divide by 4. For other sizes of prairie points, begin with a fabric strip twice as wide as the "square" you want to work with. —Liz

1. Cut enough 8"-wide strips of fabric to equal the perimeter of the quilt plus about 15". Press in half lengthwise, wrong sides facing.

2. Unfold fabric. Beginning 2" from one end of strip, rotary-cut from raw edge to, but not through, the fold. Cut away the 2"-wide rectangle. Continue making cuts up to the fold at 4" intervals. Rotate strip and begin making cuts at 4" intervals that alternate with those on the opposite edge (Photo A). Cut away any uneven end.

3. Turn strip wrong side up. Fold each square in half diagonally, bringing corner of square toward you, and press. Fold in half diagonally again, folding corner of triangle away from you, and press (Photo B).

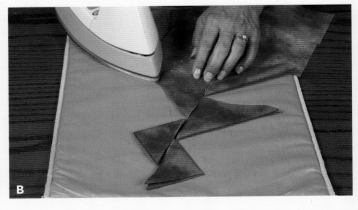

4. For a traditional tucked arrangement, slip open edge of a triangle from one side of the lengthwise fold around the folded edge of triangle from the opposite side so that they overlap (Photo C). For an arrangement we call "peaks and valleys," simply fold points on the left of lengthwise fold over those on the right (Photo D).

5. For either arrangement, machine-stitch about ⅛" from long edge to secure folds *(Photo E)*.

6. Pin strips of prairie points to right side of unquilted quilt top and stitch in place, easing as needed to bring folded edges together in corners *(Photo F)*.

7. After quilting, trim backing and batting even with raw edge of quilt top. Trim away an additional ¼" of batting. Turn prairie points so they face out from quilt, bringing raw edge of quilt top to inside. Turn under ¼" on quilt back. Blind-stitch folded edge of quilt back to prairie points, concealing machine stitching *(Photo G)*.

Two Color Continuous Prairie Points

You'll love this clever method for making continuous prairie points with two alternating fabrics.

Our instructions are for making prairie points from 3½" "squares." These will fit perfectly if the dimensions of your quilt divide by 3.5. For other sizes of prairie points, piece two fabric strips to make a strip twice as wide as the "square" you want to work with. Strip widths from 4"–8" wide for 2"–4" "squares" give nice proportions for prairie points. —Liz

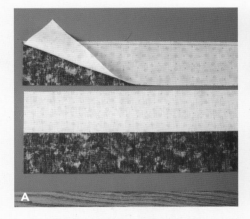

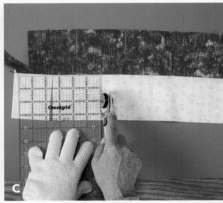

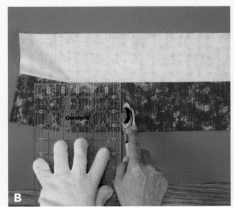

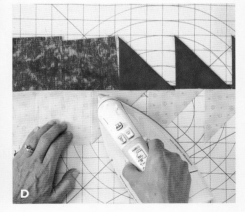

1. Cut enough 3¾"-wide strips of each of 2 fabrics to equal the perimeter of the quilt plus about 15". Join 1 strip of each color, **wrong** sides facing, with a ¼" seam. Press strips open *(Photo A)*.

2. Beginning 3½" from one end of strip, rotary-cut from raw edge to, but not through, the seam *(Photo B)*. Continue making cuts up to the seam at 3½" intervals. Rotate strip and begin making cuts at 3½" intervals that alternate with those on the opposite edge *(Photo C)*. Remove any uneven end pieces.

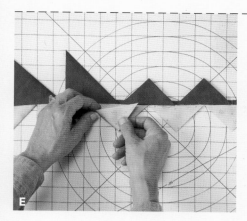

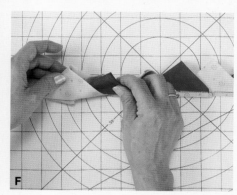

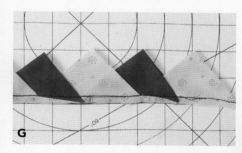

3. Turn strip wrong side up. Fold each square in half diagonally, bringing corner of square toward center, and press *(Photo D)*. Fold in half diagonally again, folding corner of triangle to center *(Photo E)*, and press.

4. For a traditional tucked arrangement, slip open edge of a triangle from one side of the seam around the folded edge of triangle from the opposite side so that they overlap *(Photo F)*.

5. Machine-stitch about ⅛" inside seam line to secure folds *(Photo G)*.

6. Pin strips of prairie points to right side of unquilted quilt top and stitch in place *(Photo H)*. Ease as needed to bring folded edges together in corners.

7. After quilting, trim backing and batting even with raw edge of quilt top. Trim away an additional ¼" of batting. Turn prairie points so they face out from quilt, bringing raw edge of quilt top to inside. Turn under ¼" on quilt back. Blindstitch folded edge of quilt back to prairie points, concealing machine stitching *(Photo I)*.

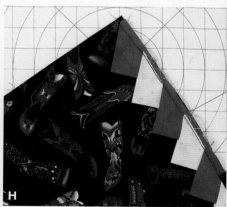

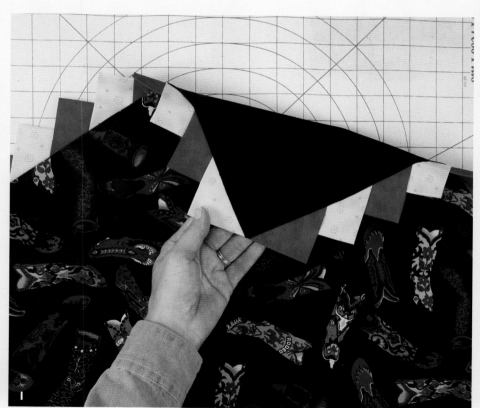

Schoolhouse Rock

When her mother-in-law retired from an elementary school teaching career that spanned decades, Lauren Caswell Brooks knew a quilt would be the perfect way to commemorate the event. She had friends and family sign muslin strips at the retirement party and then used them in the blocks and borders of this quilt.

MATERIALS

3 fat eighths★ assorted gold door/window fabrics

6 fat eighths★ assorted house fabrics

3 fat eighths★ roof fabrics

¾ yard muslin for block backgrounds and main part of pencil

18 (2½") squares assorted tan prints for pencil wood #1

1 (1" × 18") strip brown for pencil lead #2

1 fat eighth★ pink for pencil eraser

12 fat eighths★ bright prints for block sashing

1 fat eighth★ bright print for pencil border ends

1 yard blue print for sashing

1¼ yards red print for outer border and binding

Tracing Paper

3 yards backing

Twin-size batting

★ Fat eighth = 9" × 20"

PROJECT RATING: INTERMEDIATE

Finished Size: 49½" × 61½"

Blocks: 12 (10") framed Schoolhouse blocks, 18 (1¾" × 8") Pencil blocks

Cutting

Measurements include ¼" seam allowances. Border strips are exact length needed. You may want to make them longer to allow for piecing variations.

From each door/window fabric, cut:

- 4 sets of
  - 1 (2" × 3") piece for #1 door.
  - 2 (1¾" × 2¼") pieces for #2 and #4 windows.

> ### Sew **Smart**™
> It is a good idea to cut fabric pieces you will use for foundation piecing generously. We have allowed for this in these instructions. Larger pieces are easier to position and sew.
> —Marianne

From each house fabric, cut:

- 2 sets of
  - 2 (1¼" × 3") pieces for #2 and #3 house front.
  - 1 (1¾" × 3") piece for #4 house front.
  - 3 (1¾" × 2¼") pieces for #1, #3, and #5 house side pieces.
  - 2 (1½" × 4½") pieces for #6 and #7 house side pieces.
  - 2 (1" × 4") pieces for #8 house side and #3 roof divider pieces.
  - 1 (2" × 2") piece for #1 chimney piece.

From each roof fabric, cut:

- 4 sets of
  - 1 (5" × 5") piece for #4 side roof piece.
  - 1 (3½") square for #1 front roof piece.

From muslin, cut:

- 3 (1¾"-wide) strips. Cut strips into 12 (1¾" × 2") rectangles for #2 sky pieces and 12 (1¾" × 4¾") rectangles for #3 sky pieces in chimney row.

- 5 (2"-wide) strips. From strips, cut 24 (2" × 3½") rectangles for #2 and #5 sky pieces in roof row and 36 (2" × 3") rectangles for #3 and #4 pencil point background pieces.
- 3 (2¼"-wide) strips. From strips, cut 18 (2¼" × 5") pieces for main part of pencil.

From brown, cut:
- 18 (1") squares for pencil lead.

From pink, cut:
- 18 (2¼") squares for pencil erasers.

From each bright print, cut:
- 2 (2½" × 20") strips. From strips, cut 2 (2½" × 10½") side strips and 2 (2½" × 6½") top and bottom strips for block sashing.

From bright print for pencil border ends, cut:
- 3 (2¼" × 20") strips. From strips, cut 4 (2¼" × 5½") rectangles for side pencil borders and 4 (2¼" × 5¼") rectangles for pencil top and bottom borders.

From blue print, cut:
- 3 (2½"-wide) strips. From strips, cut 8 (2½" × 10½") vertical sashing strips.
- 5 (2½"-wide) strips. From strips, cut 5 (2½" × 34½") horizontal sashing strips.
- 3 (2½"-wide) strips. Piece strips to make 2 (2½" × 50½") side borders.

From red print, cut:
- 6 (4½"-wide) strips. Piece strips to make 2 (4½" × 54") side borders and 2 (4½" × 50") top and bottom borders.
- 6 (2¼"-wide) strips for binding.

Schoolhouse Block Assembly

Note: Refer to Schoolhouse Block Assembly Diagram throughout. See *Sew Easy: Paper Foundation Piecing* on page 37.

1. Photocopy or trace foundation patterns on page 124 for house front, house side, roof row, and chimney row. You will need 12 sets, 1 for each block.

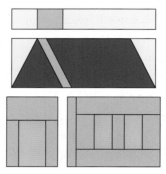

Schoolhouse Block Assembly Diagram

> **Sew Smart™**
> Foundation patterns are reversed so house will face left after foundation piecing is completed.
> —Liz

2. To make house front, choose 1 gold #1 door piece and matching house front #2 , #3 and #4 pieces.
3. Center #1 door piece right side up on back of house front foundation, covering area 1 and seam allowances. Place #2 house front piece right sides together with #1 door piece, aligning raw edges and allowing paired pieces to extend ¼" beyond seam line between areas 1 and 2 to allow for seam allowances. Using a short machine stitch, stitch along line between areas 1 and 2. Trim seam allowance to ¼" if needed. Open out #2 house front piece and finger press

so that area 2 and seam allowance are covered. Repeat on opposite side with #3 house front piece. In a similar manner, add #4 house front piece along top edge. Using rotary cutter and ruler, trim outer edges even with seam allowance line around foundation to complete house front section.

4. In similar manner, make house side section. Pieces #2 and #4 are windows; all others are house pieces and should match the ones used in the house front section.
5. Join house front to house side to complete bottom row of Schoolhouse block.
6. In a similar manner, make roof row. Pieces #1 and #4 are roof fabric, #3 is house fabric, and #2 and #5 are muslin background pieces. Add roof row to top edge of bottom house row.
7. Make chimney row. Piece #1 is house fabric; #2 and #3 are muslin background pieces.
8. Add chimney row to top of roof row to complete 1 Schoolhouse.
9. Join 1 (2½" × 6½") sashing strip to top and bottom of block. Add 1 (2½" × 10½") sashing strip to each side to complete 1 framed Schoolhouse block as shown in *Schoolhouse Block Diagram*. Remove paper from back of block.
10. Make 12 framed Schoolhouse blocks.

Pencil Block Assembly

1. Trace or photocopy pencil point foundation pattern on page 123. Make 18 foundations, 1 for each Pencil block.
2. Using foundation piecing technique, place 1 brown #2 lead piece atop

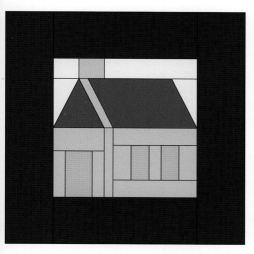

Schoolhouse Block Diagram

1 tan #1 pencil wood piece and stitch. Continue with muslin #3 and #4 background pieces. Trim excess fabric on outsides of foundation pattern even with seam allowance line. Remove paper foundation.

3. Referring to *Pencil Block Assembly Diagram*, add eraser square to 1 end of main pencil piece. Add pencil point to opposite end to complete 1 Pencil block as shown in *Pencil Block Diagram*.

4. Make 18 Pencil blocks.

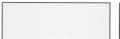

Pencil Block Assembly Diagram

Pencil Block Diagram

Sew Smart™

For fun, embroider the name of a school friend in each pencil with red embroidery floss. —Liz

Quilt Assembly

1. Referring to photograph on page 125, lay out 12 blocks, 8 vertical sashing strips, 5 horizontal sashing strips, and 2 blue side borders as shown.

2. Join 3 Schoolhouse blocks and 2 vertical sashing strips into 1 horizontal row. Make 4 rows.

3. Join 5 horizontal sashing strips and 4 horizontal block rows, alternating types.

4. Add blue side borders to opposite sides of quilt top to complete center section.

5. Join 5 Pencil blocks as shown. Add 1 bright print (2¼" × 5½") rectangle to each end of border. Add border to 1 side of quilt top. Repeat to make and add a border to opposite side of quilt top.

6. Join 4 Pencil blocks as shown. Add 1 bright print (2¼" × 5¼") rectangle to each end of border. Add border to top of quilt top. Repeat to make and add a border to bottom of quilt top.

7. Add red side borders. Add red top and bottom borders.

Quilting and Finishing

1. Divide backing into 2 (1½-yard) lengths. Trim 1 piece to 30" wide. Join 30" piece to bottom of larger piece; press seam allowance toward narrow piece. Seam will run horizontally across quilt back. Remaining piece is extra and may be used to make a hanging sleeve.

2. Layer backing, batting, and quilt top; baste. Quilt as desired. Quilt shown was quilted with apples in blocks and meander quilting in pencil border. Outer border features lines of people holding hands.

3. Join 2¼"-wide red print strips into 1 continuous piece for straight-grain French-fold binding. Add binding to quilt.

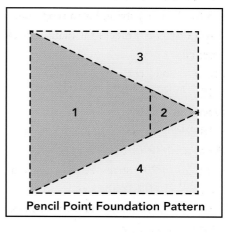

Pencil Point Foundation Pattern

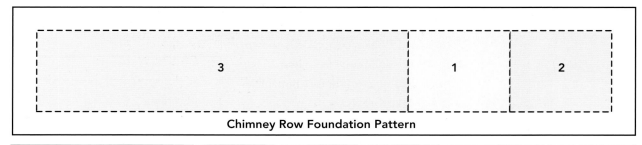

Chimney Row Foundation Pattern

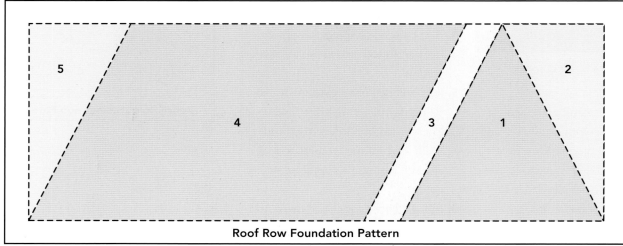

Roof Row Foundation Pattern

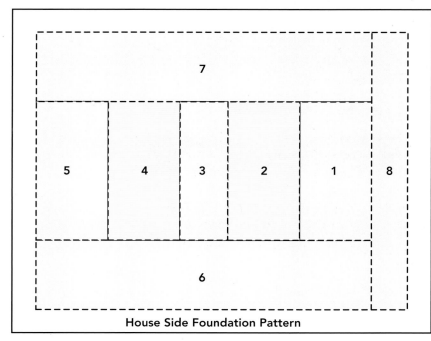

House Side Foundation Pattern

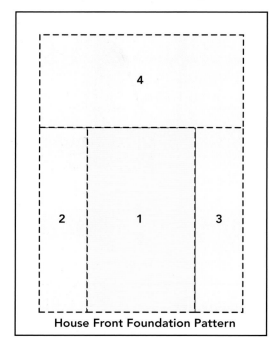

House Front Foundation Pattern

DESIGNER

Lauren Coswell Brooks is the former features editor for *For the Love of Quilting*. She enjoys stitching quilts in her free time and especially likes making quilts for babies and children. ✳

Christmas Memories

With just two foundation-pieced blocks and a little machine appliqué, this is a quick wallhanging to make for a gift or for yourself.

Size: 36" × 17"
Blocks: 2 (6½" × 9") Tree blocks
1 (11" × 9") House block

MATERIALS

1 fat quarter★★ light blue print for
block background
1 fat eighth★ dark blue print for
Roof and Door
1 fat eighth★ green print #1 for
Tree blocks and sashing
¼ yard green print #2 for Tree
blocks and inner border
1 fat eighth★ green print #3 for
Tree blocks
⅜ yard red print for House block
and binding
4" square gold solid for Windows
⅜ yard gold print for outer border
1 fat eighth★ brown print for blocks
Paper for foundations
Paper-backed fusible web
⅝ yard backing fabric
Craft-size quilt batting
★★fat quarter = 18" × 20"
★fat eighth = 9" × 20"

Cutting

Measurements include ¼" seam allowances. Border strips are exact length needed. You may want to make them longer to allow for piecing variations. Foundation patterns are on pages 130–131. Follow manufacturer's instructions for using fusible web. For step-by-step photos and a video, see *Sew Easy: Fusible Web Appliqué* at www.fonsandporter.com/fusiblewebapp.

From light blue print fat quarter, cut:
• 1 (1¾"-wide) strip. From strip,
cut 4 (1¾" × 3⅜") H rectangles and
2 (1¾" × 1½") D rectangles.
• 3 (1½"-wide) strips. From strips, cut
3 (1½" × 9½") F rectangles, and
1 (1½" × 5") E rectangle.
• 1 B.
• 1 B reversed.

From dark blue print, cut:
• 1 Roof.
• 1 Door.

From green print #1 fat eighth, cut:
• 2 (1½"-wide) strips. From strips, cut
4 (1½" × 9½") F rectangles.

From green print #2, cut:

- 2 (1½"-wide) strips. From strips, cut 2 (1½" × 28½") top and bottom inner borders and 2 (1½" × 9½") side inner borders.

From green print #3 fat eighth, cut:

- 1 (1½"-wide) strip. From strip, cut 4 (1½") C squares.

From red print, cut:

- 1 (5"-wide) strip. From strip, cut 1 (5" × 9½") A rectangle.
- 3 (2¼"-wide) strips for binding.

From gold solid, cut:

- 2 Windows.

From gold print, cut:

- 3 (3½"-wide) strips. From strips, cut 2 (3½" × 36½") top and bottom outer borders and 2 (3½" × 11½") side outer borders.

From brown print fat eighth, cut:

- 1 (1½"-wide) strip. From strip, cut 2 (1½") C squares.
- 1 (1¼"-wide) strip. From strip, cut 2 (1¼" × 1¾") G rectangles.

House Block Assembly

1. Referring to *House Block Assembly Diagrams*, join brown print C squares, light blue print D rectangles, and light blue print E rectangle as shown to make Chimney Unit.

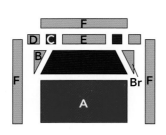

House Block Assembly Diagrams

2. Join dark blue print Roof, light blue print B, and light blue print B reversed to make Roof Unit.

3. Lay out 3 light blue print F rectangles, Chimney Unit, Roof Unit, and red print A rectangle as shown. Join to make House block background.

4. Position Door and Windows atop block background; fuse in place. Machine appliqué using satin stitch to complete House block (*House Block Diagram*).

House Block Diagram

Tree Block Assembly

For instructions on foundation piecing see *Sew Easy: Paper Foundation Piecing* on page 37.

1. Trace or photocopy 2 Tree Unit foundations from pattern on page 130.

2. Referring to *Tree Unit Diagram*, foundation piece units in numerical order. Make 2 Tree Units.

Tree Unit Diagram

3. Join 1 brown print G rectangle and 2 light blue print H rectangles as shown in *Tree Block Assembly Diagram*. Make 2 Trunk Units.

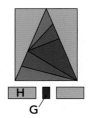

Tree Block Assembly Diagram

4. Join 1 Tree Unit and 1 Trunk Unit to complete 1 Tree block (*Tree Block Diagram*). Make 2 Tree blocks.

Tree Block Diagram

Quilt Assembly

1. Lay out blocks and green print #1 F rectangles as shown in *Quilt Top Assembly Diagram*. Join to complete quilt center.

2. Add green print #2 side inner borders to quilt center.

3. Add 1 green print #3 C square to each end of top and bottom inner borders. Add borders to quilt.

4. Add gold print side outer borders to quilt center. Add gold print top and bottom outer borders to quilt.

Finishing

1. Layer backing, batting, and quilt top; baste. Quilt as desired. Quilt shown was quilted with tree designs in tree blocks, bricks and shingles in house block, and meandering in block backgrounds and borders (*Quilting Diagram*).

3. Join 2¼"-wide red print strips into 1 continuous piece for straight-grain French-fold binding. Add binding to quilt.

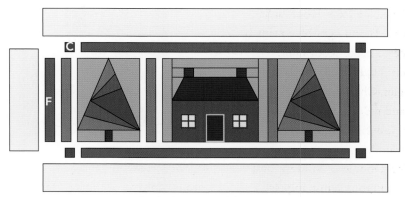

Quilt Top Assembly Diagram

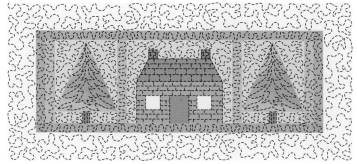

Quilting Diagram

DESIGNER

Judy Hansen's passion for art and all things sewing has led her to a place in her life that is full of both. She is owner of the Quilt Shop in DeLand, Florida, and has authored three books on quilting and over seventy-five quilt patterns. Her latest love affair is designing fabric. ✳

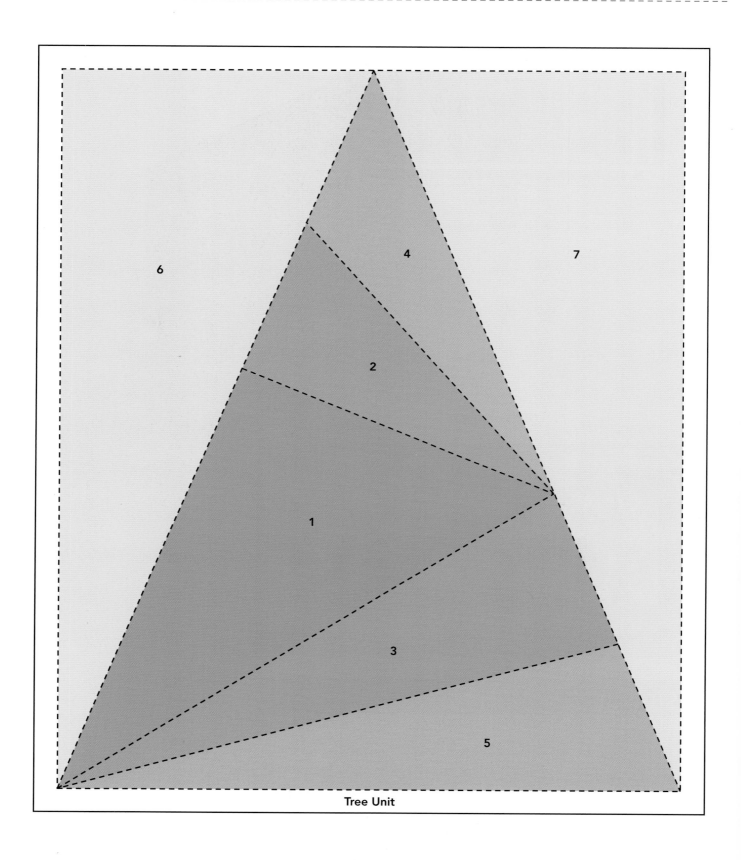

Tree Unit

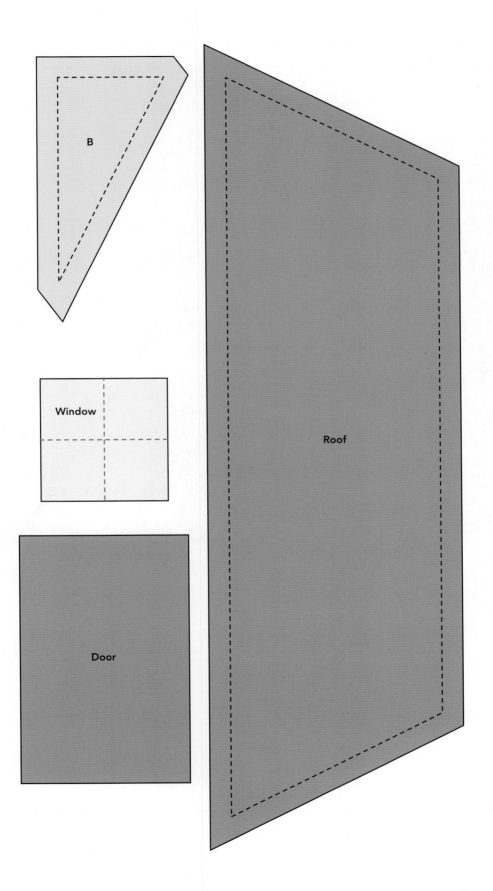

General Instructions

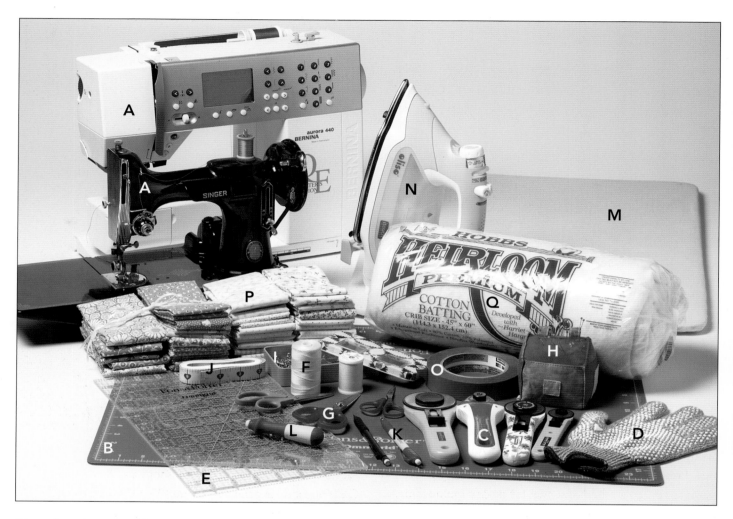

Basic Supplies

You'll need a **sewing machine (A)** in good working order to construct patchwork blocks, join blocks together, add borders, and machine quilt. We encourage you to purchase a machine from a local dealer, who can help you with service in the future, rather than from a discount store. Another option may be to borrow a machine from a friend or family member. If the machine has not been used in a while, have it serviced by a local dealer to make sure it is in good working order. If you need an extension cord, one with a surge protector is a good idea.

A **rotary cutting mat (B)** is essential for accurate and safe rotary cutting. Purchase one that is no smaller than 18" × 24".

Rotary cutting mats are made of "self-healing" material that can be used over and over.

A **rotary cutter (C)** is a cutting tool that looks like a pizza cutter, and has a very sharp blade. We recommend starting with a standard size 45mm rotary cutter. Always lock or close your cutter when it is not in use, and keep it out of the reach of children.

A **safety glove** (also known as a *Klutz Glove)* **(D)** is also recommended. Wear your safety glove on the hand that is holding the ruler in place. Because it is made of cut-resistant material, the safety glove protects your non-cutting hand from accidents that can occur if your cutting hand slips while cutting.

An acrylic **ruler (E)** is used in combination with your cutting mat and rotary cutter. We recommend the Fons & Porter

8" × 14" ruler, but a 6" × 12" ruler is another good option. You'll need a ruler with inch, quarter-inch, and eighth-inch markings that show clearly for ease of measuring. Choose a ruler with 45-degree-angle, 30-degree-angle, and 60-degree-angle lines marked on it as well.

Since you will be using 100% cotton fabric for your quilts, use **cotton or cotton-covered polyester thread (F)** for piecing and quilting. Avoid 100% polyester thread, as it tends to snarl.

Keep a pair of small **scissors (G)** near your sewing machine for cutting threads.

Thin, good quality **straight pins (H)** are preferred by quilters. The pins included with pin cushions are normally too thick to use for piecing, so discard them. Purchase a box of nickel-plated brass **safety pins** size #1 **(I)** to use for pin-basting the layers of your quilt together for machine quilting.

Invest in a 120"-long dressmaker's **measuring tape (J)**. This will come in handy when making borders for your quilt.

A 0.7–0.9mm mechanical **pencil (K)** works well for marking on your fabric.

Invest in a quality sharp **seam ripper (L)**. Every quilter gets well-acquainted with her seam ripper!

Set up an **ironing board (M)** and **iron (N)** in your sewing area. Pressing yardage before cutting, and pressing patchwork seams as you go are both essential for quality quiltmaking. Select an iron that has steam capability.

Masking **tape (O)** or painter's tape works well to mark your sewing machine so you can sew an accurate ¼" seam. You will also use tape to hold your backing fabric taut as you prepare your quilt sandwich for machine quilting.

The most exciting item that you will need for quilting is **fabric (P)**. Quilters generally prefer 100% cotton fabrics for their quilts. This fabric is woven from cotton threads, and has a lengthwise and a crosswise grain. The term "bias" is used to describe the diagonal grain of the fabric. If you make a 45-degree angle cut through a square of cotton fabric, the cut edges will be bias edges, which are quite stretchy. As you learn more quiltmaking techniques, you'll learn how bias can work to your advantage or disadvantage.

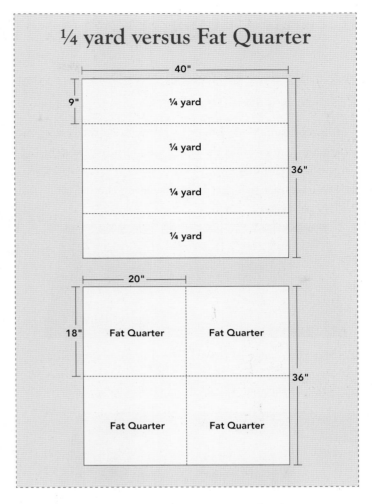

¼ yard versus Fat Quarter

Fabric is sold by the yard at quilt shops and fabric stores. Quilting fabric is generally about 40"–44" wide, so a yard is about 40" wide by 36" long. As you collect fabrics to build your own personal stash, you will buy yards, half yards (about 18" × 40"), quarter yards (about 9" × 40"), as well as other lengths.

Many quilt shops sell "fat quarters," a special cut favored by quilters. A fat quarter is created by cutting a half yard down the fold line into two 18" × 20" pieces (fat quarters) that are sold separately. Quilters like the nearly square shape of the fat quarter because it is more useful than the narrow regular quarter yard cut.

Batting (Q) is the filler between quilt top and backing that makes your quilt a quilt. It can be cotton, polyester, cotton-polyester blend, wool, silk, or other natural materials, such as bamboo or corn. Make sure the batting you buy is at least six inches wider and six inches longer than your quilt top.

Accurate Cutting

Measuring and cutting accuracy are important for successful quilting. Measure at least twice, and cut once!

Cut strips across the fabric width unless directed otherwise.

Cutting for patchwork usually begins with cutting strips, which are then cut into smaller pieces. First, cut straight strips from a fat quarter:

1. Fold fat quarter in half with selvage edge at the top (*Photo A*).

2. Straighten edge of fabric by placing ruler atop fabric, aligning one of the lines on ruler with selvage edge of fabric (*Photo B*). Cut along right edge of ruler.

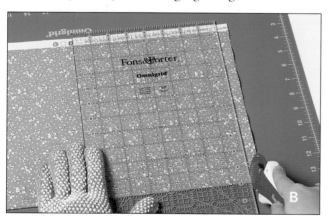

3. Rotate fabric, and use ruler to measure from cut edge to desired strip width (*Photo C*). Measurements in instructions include ¼" seam allowances.

4. After cutting the required number of strips, cut strips into squares and label them.

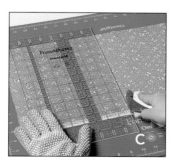

Setting up Your Sewing Machine

Sew Accurate ¼" Seams

Standard seam width for patchwork and quiltmaking is ¼". Some machines come with a patchwork presser foot, also known as a quarter-inch foot. If your machine doesn't have a quarter-inch foot, you may be able to purchase one from a dealer. Or, you can create a quarter-inch seam guide on your machine using masking tape or painter's tape.

Place an acrylic ruler on your sewing machine bed under the presser foot. Slowly turn handwheel until the tip of the needle barely rests atop the ruler's quarter-inch mark (*Photo A*). Make sure the lines on the ruler are parallel to the lines on the machine throat plate. Place tape on the machine bed along edge of ruler (*Photo B*).

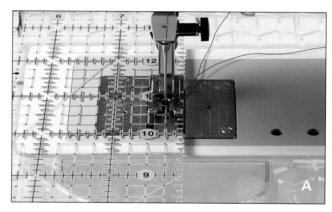

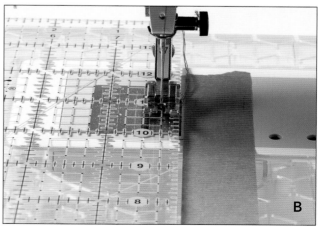

Take a Simple Seam Test

Seam accuracy is critical to machine piecing, so take this simple test once you have your quarter-inch presser foot on your machine or have created a tape guide.

Place 2 (2½") squares right sides together, and sew with a scant ¼" seam. Open squares and finger press seam. To finger press, with right sides facing you, press the seam to one side with your fingernail. Measure across pieces, raw edge to raw edge (*Photo C*). If they measure 4½", you have passed the test! Repeat the test as needed to make sure you can confidently sew a perfect ¼" seam.

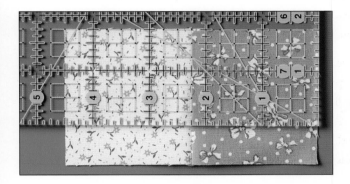

Sewing Comfortably

Other elements that promote pleasant sewing are good lighting, a comfortable chair, background music—and chocolate! Good lighting promotes accurate sewing. The better you can see what you are working on, the better your results. A comfortable chair enables you to sew for longer periods of time. An office chair with a good back rest and adjustable height works well. Music helps keep you relaxed. Chocolate is, for many quilters, simply a necessity.

Tips for Patchwork and Pressing

As you sew more patchwork, you'll develop your own shortcuts and favorite methods. Here are a few favored by many quilters:

● As you join patchwork units to form rows, and join rows to form blocks, press seams in opposite directions from row to row whenever possible (*Photo A*). By pressing seams one direction in the first row and the opposite direction in the next row, you will often create seam allowances that abut when rows are joined (*Photo B*). Abutting or nesting seams are ideal for forming perfectly matched corners on the right side of your quilt blocks and quilt top. Such pressing is not always possible, so don't worry if you end up with seam allowances facing the same direction as you join units.

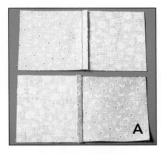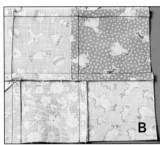

● Sew on and off a small, folded fabric square to prevent bobbin thread from bunching at throat plate (*Photo C*). You'll also save thread, which means fewer stops to wind bobbins, and fewer hanging threads to be snipped. Repeated use of the small piece of fabric gives it lots of thread "legs," so some quilters call it a spider.

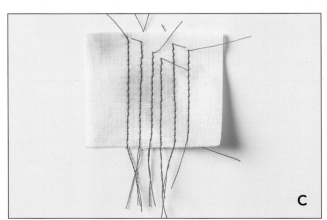

● Chain piece patchwork to reduce the amount of thread you use, and minimize the number and length of threads you need to trim from patchwork. Without cutting threads at the end of a seam, take 3–4 stitches without any fabric under the needle, creating a short thread chain approximately ⅛" long (*Photo D*). Repeat until you have a long line of pieces. Remove chain from machine, clip threads between units, and press seams.

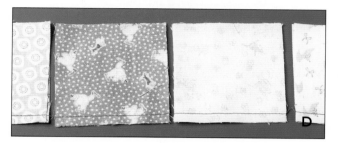

● Trim off tiny triangle tips (sometimes called dog ears) created when making triangle-square units (*Photo E*). Trimming triangles reduces bulk and makes patchwork units and blocks lie flatter. Though no one will see the back of your quilt top once it's quilted, a neat back free of dangling threads and patchwork points is the mark of a good quilter. Also, a smooth, flat quilt top is easier to quilt, whether by hand or machine.

● Careful pressing will make your patchwork neat and crisp, and will help make your finished quilt top lie flat. Ironing and pressing are two different skills. Iron fabric to remove wrinkles using a back and forth, smoothing motion. Press patchwork and quilt blocks by raising and gently lowering the iron atop your work. After sewing a patchwork unit, first press the seam with the unit closed, pressing to set, or embed, the stitching. Setting the seam this way will help produce straight, crisp seams. Open the unit and press on the right side with the seam toward the darkest

fabric, being careful to not form a pleat in your seam, and carefully pressing the patchwork flat.

● Many quilters use finger pressing to open and flatten seams of small units before pressing with an iron. To finger press, open patchwork unit with right side of fabric facing you. Run your fingernail firmly along seam, making sure unit is fully open with no pleat.

● Careful use of steam in your iron will make seams and blocks crisp and flat (*Photo F*). Aggressive ironing can stretch blocks out of shape, and is a common pitfall for new quilters.

Adding Borders

Follow these simple instructions to make borders that fit perfectly on your quilt.

1. Find the length of your quilt by measuring through the quilt center, not along the edges, since the edges may have stretched. Take 3 measurements and average them to determine the length to cut your side borders (*Diagram A*). Cut 2 side borders this length.

2. Fold border strips in half to find center. Pinch to create crease mark or place a pin at center. Fold quilt top in half crosswise to find center of side. Attach side borders to quilt center by pinning them at the ends and the center, and easing in any fullness. If quilt edge is a bit longer than border, pin and sew with border on top; if border is

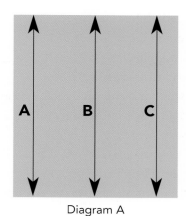

Diagram A

A _____

B _____

C _____

TOTAL _____

÷3 _____

AVERAGE
LENGTH _____

slightly longer than quilt top, pin and sew with border on the bottom. Machine feed dogs will ease in the fullness of the longer piece. Press seams toward borders.

3. Find the width of your quilt by measuring across the quilt and side borders (*Diagram B*). Take 3 measurements and average them to determine the length to cut your top and bottom borders. Cut 2 borders this length.

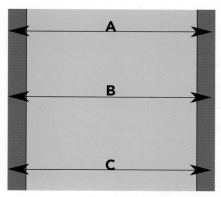

Diagram B

4. Mark centers of borders and top and bottom edges of quilt top. Attach top and bottom borders to quilt, pinnning at ends and center, and easing in any fullness (*Diagram C*). Press seams toward borders.

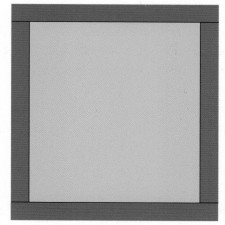

Diagram C

5. Gently steam press entire quilt top on one side and then the other. When pressing on wrong side, trim off any loose threads.

Joining Border Strips

Not all quilts have borders, but they are a nice complement to a quilt top. If your border is longer than 40", you will need to join 2 or more strips to make a border the required length. You can join border strips with either a straight seam parallel to the ends of the strips (*Photo A* on page 138), or with a diagonal seam. For the diagonal seam method, place one border strip perpendicular to another strip, rights sides facing (*Photo B*). Stitch diagonally across strips as shown. Trim seam allowance to ¼". Press seam open (*Photo C*).

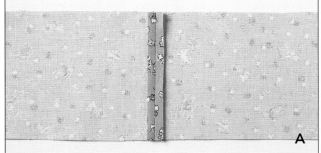

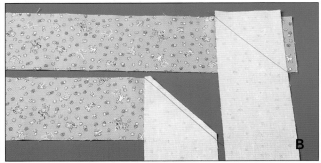

Quilting Your Quilt

Quilters today joke that there are three ways to quilt a quilt— by hand, by machine, or by check. Some enjoy making quilt tops so much, they prefer to hire a professional machine quilter to finish their work. The Split Nine Patch baby quilt shown at left has simple machine quilting that you can do yourself.

Decide what color thread will look best on your quilt top before choosing your backing fabric. A thread color that will blend in with the quilt top is a good choice for beginners. Choose backing fabric that will blend with your thread as well. A print fabric is a good choice for hiding less-than-perfect machine quilting. The backing fabric must be at least 3"–4" larger than your quilt top on all 4 sides. For example: if your quilt top measures 44" × 44", your backing needs to be at least 50" × 50". If your quilt top is 80" × 96", then your backing fabric needs to be at least 86" × 102".

For quilt tops 36" wide or less, use a single width of fabric for the backing. Buy enough length to allow adequate margin at quilt edges, as noted above. When your quilt is wider than 36", one option is to use 60"-, 90"-, or 108"-wide fabric for the quilt backing. Because fabric selection is limited for wide fabrics, quilters generally piece the quilt backing from 44/45"-wide fabric. Plan on 40"–42" of usable fabric width when estimating how much fabric to purchase. Plan your piecing strategy to avoid having a seam along the vertical or horizontal center of the quilt.

For a quilt 37"–60" wide, a backing with horizontal seams is usually the most economical use of fabric. For example, for a quilt 50" × 70", vertical seams would require 152", or 4¼ yards, of 44/45"-wide fabric (76" + 76" = 152"). Horizontal seams would require 112", or 3¼ yards (56" + 56" = 112").

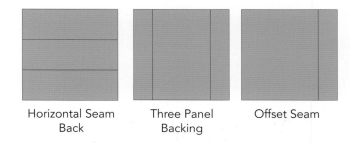

Horizontal Seam Back   Three Panel Backing   Offset Seam

For a quilt 61"–80" wide, most quilters piece a three-panel backing, with vertical seams, from two lengths of fabric. Cut one of the pieces in half lengthwise, and sew the halves to opposite sides of the wider panel. Press the seams away from the center panel.

For a quilt 81"–120" wide, you will need three lengths of fabric, plus extra margin. For example, for a quilt 108" × 108", purchase at least 342", or 9½ yards, of 44/45"-wide fabric (114" + 114" + 114" = 342").

For a three-panel backing, pin the selvage edge of the center panel to the selvage edge of the side panel, with edges aligned and right sides facing. Machine stitch with a ½" seam. Trim seam allowances to ¼", trimming off the selvages from both panels at once. Press the seam away from the center of the quilt. Repeat on other side of center panel.

For a two-panel backing, join panels in the same manner as above, and press the seam to one side.

Create a "quilt sandwich" by layering your backing, batting, and quilt top. Find the crosswise center of the backing fabric by folding it in half. Mark with a pin on each side. Lay backing down on a table or floor, wrong side up. Tape corners and edges of backing to the surface with masking or painter's tape so that backing is taut (*Photo A*).

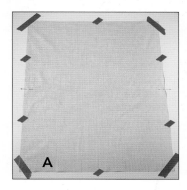

Fold batting in half crosswise and position it atop backing fabric, centering folded edge at center of backing (*Photo B*). Unfold batting and smooth it out atop backing (*Photo C*).

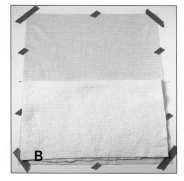
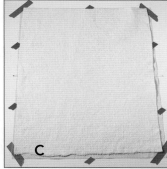

In the same manner, fold the quilt top in half crosswise and center it atop backing and batting (*Photo D*). Unfold top and smooth it out atop batting (*Photo E*).

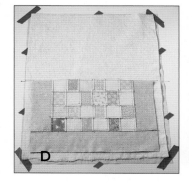

Use safety pins to pin baste the layers (*Photo F*). Pins should be about a fist width apart. A special tool, called a Kwik Klip, or a grapefruit spoon makes closing the pins easier. As you slide a pin through all three layers, slide the point of the pin into one of the tool's grooves. Push on the tool to help close the pin.

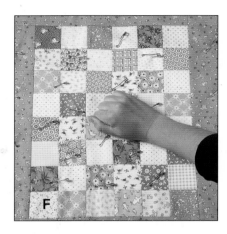

For straight line quilting, install an even feed or walking foot on your machine. This presser foot helps all three layers of your quilt move through the machine evenly without bunching.

Walking Foot   Stitching "in the ditch"

An easy way to quilt your first quilt is to stitch "in the ditch" along seam lines. No marking is needed for this type of quilting.

Binding Your Quilt

Preparing Binding

Strips for quilt binding may be cut either on the straight of grain or on the bias.

1. Measure the perimeter of your quilt and add approximately 24" to allow for mitered corners and finished ends.
2. Cut the number of strips necessary to achieve desired length. We like to cut binding strips 2¼" wide.
3. Join your strips with diagonal seams into 1 continuous piece (*Photo A*). Press the seams open. (See page 142 for instructions for the diagonal seams method of joining strips.)

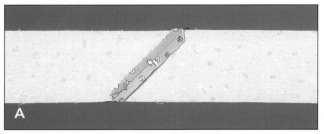

4. Press your binding in half lengthwise, with wrong sides facing, to make French-fold binding (*Photo B*).

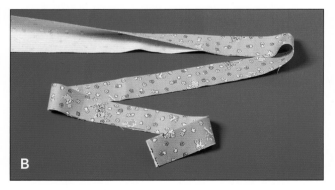

Attaching Binding

Attach the binding to your quilt using an even-feed or walking foot. This prevents puckering when sewing through the three layers.

1. Choose beginning point along one side of quilt. Do not start at a corner. Match the two raw edges of the binding strip to the raw edge of the quilt top. The folded edge

will be free and to left of seam line (*Photo C*). Leave 12" or longer tail of binding strip dangling free from beginning point. Stitch, using ¼" seam, through all layers.

2. For mitered corners, stop stitching ¼" from corner; backstitch, and remove quilt from sewing machine (*Photo D*). Place a pin ¼" from corner to mark where you will stop stitching.

Rotate quilt quarter turn and fold binding straight up, away from corner, forming 45-degree-angle fold (*Photo E*).

Bring binding straight down in line with next edge to be sewn, leaving top fold even with raw edge of previously sewn side (*Photo F*). Begin stitching at top edge, sewing through all layers (*Photo G*).

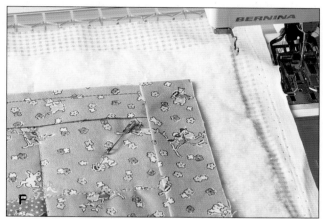

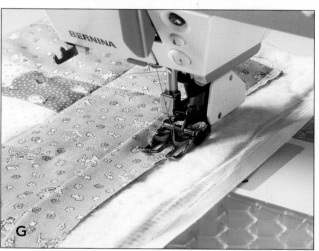

3. To finish binding, stop stitching about 8" away from starting point, leaving about a 12" tail at end (*Photo H*). Bring beginning and end of binding to center of 8" opening and fold each back, leaving about ¼" space

between the two folds of binding (*Photo I*). (Allowing this ¼" extra space is critical, as binding tends to stretch when it is stitched to the quilt. If the folded ends meet at this point, your binding will be too long for the space after the ends are joined.) Crease folds of binding with your fingernail.

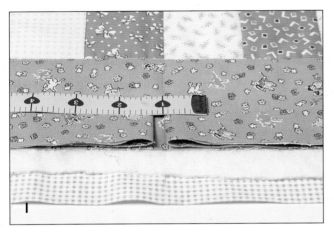

4. Open out each edge of binding and draw line across wrong side of binding on creased fold line, as shown in *Photo J*. Draw line along lengthwise fold of binding at same spot to create an X (*Photo K*).

5. With edge of ruler at marked X, line up 45-degree-angle marking on ruler with one long side of binding (*Photo L*). Draw diagonal line across binding as shown in *Photo M*.

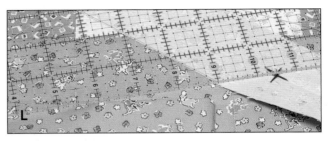

Repeat for other end of binding. Lines must angle in same direction (*Photo N*).

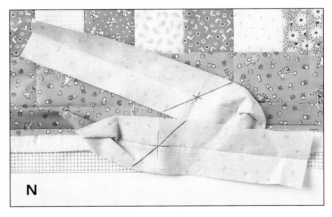

6. Pin binding ends together with right sides facing, pin-matching diagonal lines as shown in *Photo O*. Binding ends will be at right angles to each other. Machine-stitch along diagonal line, removing pins as you stitch (*Photo P*).

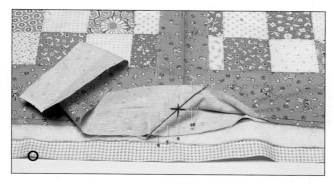

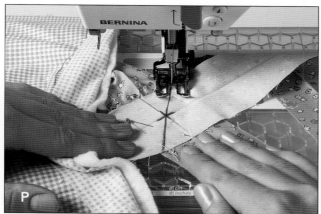

7. Lay binding against quilt to double-check that it is correct length (*Photo Q*). Trim ends of binding ¼" from diagonal seam (*Photo R*).

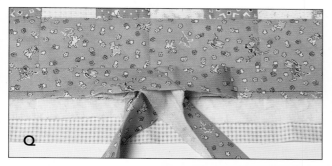

8. Finger press diagonal seam open (*Photo S*). Fold binding in half and finish stitching binding to quilt (*Photo T*).

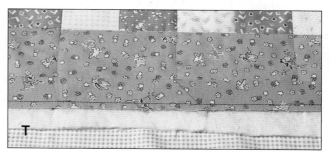

Hand Stitching Binding to Quilt Back

1. Trim any excess batting and quilt back with scissors or a rotary cutter (*Photo A*). Leave enough batting (about ⅛" beyond quilt top) to fill binding uniformly when it is turned to quilt back.

2. Bring folded edge of binding to quilt back so that it covers machine stitching. Blindstitch folded edge to quilt backing, using a few pins just ahead of stitching to hold binding in place (*Photo B*).

3. Continue stitching to corner. Fold unstitched binding from next side under, forming a 45-degree angle and a mitered corner. Stitch mitered folds on both front and back (*Photo C*).

Finishing Touches

● **Label your quilt so the recipient and future generations know who made it.** To make a label, use a fabric marking pen to write the details on a small piece of solid color fabric (*Photo A*). To make writing easier, put pieces of masking tape on the wrong side. Remove tape after writing. Use your iron to turn under ¼" on each edge, then stitch the label to the back of your quilt using a blindstitch, taking care not to sew through to quilt top.

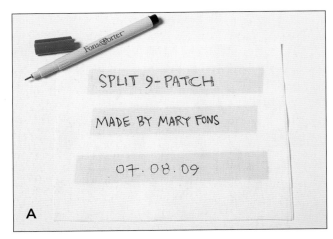

● **Take a photo of your quilt.** Keep your photos in an album or journal along with notes, fabric swatches, and other information about the quilts.

● **If your quilt is a gift, include care instructions.** Some quilt shops carry pre-printed care labels you can sew onto the quilt (*Photo B*). Or, make a care label using the method described above.